Punishment:
Theory and Practice

Punishment

Theory and Practice

Mark Tunick

UNIVERSITY OF CALIFORNIA PRESS
BERKELEY LOS ANGELES OXFORD

University of California Press
Berkeley and Los Angeles, California

University of California Press, Ltd.
Oxford, England

© 1992 by
The Regents of the University of California

Library of Congress Cataloging-in-Publication Data
Tunick, Mark.
   Punishment : theory and practice / Mark Tunick.
      p.   cm.
   Includes bibliographical references and index.
   ISBN 0-520-07737-7
   1. Punishment   I. Title.
   K5103.T86   1992
   345'.077—dc20
   [342.577]   91–32129
                                                     CIP

Printed in the United States of America

9 8 7 6 5 4 3 2 1

The paper used in this publication meets the minimum
requirements of American National Standard for
Information Sciences—Permanence of Paper for Printed
Library Materials, ANSI Z39.48-1984. ∞

Contents

Preface

Currently there is a debate about whether we should allow our prisons to be owned and operated privately. One opponent of private prisons argues, "What are the core purposes of government? Foreign affairs and domestic defense. I count corrections and detention as among the latter, and I don't think our government should contract out its core reason for being." But an internal auditor for Texas's Department of Corrections isn't persuaded: "I'm an old state bureaucrat. . . . I don't have any philosophies. If they can do it cheaper than the state can, more power to them" (*New York Times*, March 27, 1990). To the hard-nosed Texas auditor concerned with what works most efficiently, the theorist who appeals to a philosophy of what's morally right is too taken with abstractions and high-sounding principles to confront the tough choices and uncomfortable truths of the real world. The tension in this confrontation is well known, perhaps inevitable, but nevertheless disturbing; it is the tension between the theorist who stands on the "outside" talking of ideals and principles, and the practitioner who is "inside" and needs to get things done.

This is a book of theory about one of the most troubling of our social practices, legal punishment. My aim is to show how theory and practice converge. My reflections are addressed to ordinary people and to practitioners who think about and in some cases must confront the problems that emerge from this practice. As a theorist, I assume a position of critical distance. I do not take as authoritative all the existing rules and features of the practice of legal punishment; as we shall see, many of us disagree with some of those rules, or don't think certain features should be a part of the practice. I believe there is an ideal of justice underlying our practice of legal punishment, an ideal that sometimes gets obscured, lost in the shadows of the institutions of criminal law. This ideal of justice can seem beside the point to police officers, prosecutors, trial court judges, and a concerned citizenry, all facing a reality of violent and pervasive crime, overburdened courts, and overcrowded jails and prisons. I believe the theorist must adjust her ideals in light of the facts; only then may practitioners listen. But the theorist, as a theorist, is committed with her ideals sometimes to persevere in the face of a less than ideal actuality.

This book is a work of theory because it holds up ideals to the reality of our criminal justice system; but it is a work of theory also because it considers whether we should have the practice of legal punishment at all, an issue not often raised by practitioners such as judges, defense attorneys, and prosecutors, whose preoccupations inside the practice afford them little opportunity to step back and reflect on such a heady question. Addressing the question "Why punish at all?" is not a mere philosophical and intellectually edifying exercise. The answer matters practically. For if we have a compelling interpretation of why we punish, of the purpose of the practice, then from this account we might derive principles and standards that determine how we resolve the problems engaging those practitioners.

I am a theorist who is on the whole committed to the practices we have at hand. This does not mean that I am committed to overcrowded prisons, overburdened courts, and all the injustices and inefficiencies of our present criminal justice system. It means, rather, that I believe that by reflecting on the ideals implicit in the practice we have at hand we can come to implement a just practice that is already within our reach. Though aware of the need to challenge our practices, sometimes radically, I want to avoid assuming a position unconnected with or detached from this world. I am convinced that if the theorist is to make a difference to practitioners, she must understand their concerns and even share some of their commitments. I believe the theorist can do this without abandoning her critical stance. This work is addressed not only to those working within the criminal justice system, to whom I talk about topics including plea-bargaining, the insanity defense, the exclusionary rule, sentencing discretion, and the proper scope of the criminal law; but also to political and legal theorists and social critics in general, to whom I talk about the precarious balance the critic must attain between, on the one hand, commitment to ideals and, on the other hand, connection with actuality.

I have many people to thank for their help in getting me to sharpen and make clear my arguments. Foremost among them are Hanna Pitkin, who, by setting such high standards for clarity, scholarship, and intellectual integrity, has helped make me my own best critic; and Jeremy Waldron, who, with considerable energy and determination, encouraged me to formulate what I hope is a more persuasive account of why we punish. My thanks are also due to Dan Avnon, Pat Bolling, Stanley Brubaker, Alyson Cole, James Coleman, Elizabeth Collins, John Ferejohn, Jill Frank, Elisabeth Hansot, Emily Hauptmann, Norman Jacobson, Steve Krasner, Jane-Ellen Long, Dennis McEnnerney, Mike Ochoa, Susan Okin, Fred Schaefer, Jackie Stevens, Paul Thomas, and Brian Wiener; and finally, to my dearest friend, to whom I dedicate this book, Larissa.

1

Introduction

1. The Issues, External and Internal

Of all our social practices, legal punishment is one of the most troubling to us. When we—that is, the state—legally punish, we invoke our authority in order to inflict pain, deprivation, or some other form of suffering.[1] The state's power to punish legally can be the power of life and death. In Judge Roy Jones's proposal that a mother who fed her four-year-old son fatal doses of psychiatric drugs agree to sterilization in exchange for a reduction in sentence, declaring that she was "a person who no longer needs ever to have any children," could be heard the voice of God: be not fruitful, do not multiply.[2]

1. Only the state or public authority may with right legally punish: see Thomas Hobbes, *Leviathan*, ed. Michael Oakeshott (New York: Collier Books, 1962), ch. 28 ("executed by a due authority"); and Antony Flew, "The Justification of Punishment," *Philosophy*, vol. 29, no. 111 (October 1954), pp. 292–94.

2. *New York Times*, September 25, 1988. Some courts have challenged such rulings. The South Carolina Supreme Court reversed an order that a young woman who abandoned her two young sons in a sweltering apartment remain on birth control for the rest of her childbearing years, but on the grounds that this punishment was unenforceable because of the fallibility of birth control (*New York Times*, May 26, 1988). See also *Skinner v. Oklahoma*, 316 U.S. 535

We disagree about the morality of punishing at all. Legal punishment often hurts its victim, and this troubles many of us.[3] Some think legal punishment is institutionalized revenge, and that we are now above all that; we are now in an age of enlightenment, living according to humanitarian principles, and punishment is a regression to a past we have shed and that is best forgotten.[4] In this view, when we punish we go against our enlightened selves; we are no longer at home in, or comfortable with, this practice. Recently a concert promoter convicted of dealing in cocaine avoided a lengthy jail sentence by agreeing to stage a rock concert to benefit drug-treatment programs for juveniles. The concert promoter justified the laxity of his punishment: "This is a better deal for society. Locking me up and charging the taxpayers for it and possibly having me come out worse than I went in does not help anyone."[5] *This* is the enlightened response to punishment.

But not all of us accept this line; many are outraged. This man broke the law; he deserves to suffer for his wrong—he

---

(1942), in which the U.S. Supreme Court struck down Oklahoma's Habitual Criminal Sterilization Act, which authorized the sterilization of persons previously convicted and imprisoned two or more times for crimes "amounting to felonies involving moral turpitude" and thereafter convicted of such a felony and sentenced to prison.

3. On the association of punishment with pain, see, for example, Herbert Packer, *The Limits of the Criminal Sanction* (Stanford: Stanford University Press, 1968), p. 21; Edwin Sutherland and Donald Cressey, *Criminology*, 8th ed. (Philadelphia: J. B. Lippincott, 1970), p. 298; Karl Menninger, *The Crime of Punishment* (New York: Viking Press, 1966), p. 202; Immanuel Kant, *Metaphysik der Sitten*, in *Werke in Sechs Bänden*, ed. Wilhelm Weischedel, vol. 4 (1798; Darmstadt: Wissenschaftliche Buchgesellschaft, 1963), A195, B225; and Otto Kirchheimer and Georg Rusche, *Punishment and Social Structure* (New York: Russell and Russell, 1939), p. 46; but see Flew, "The Justification of Punishment," p. 292, who says punishment must be an evil or unpleasantness but need not be physically painful.

4. On punishment as institutionalized revenge see, for example, René Girard, *Violence and the Sacred*, trans. Patrick Gregory (1972; Baltimore: Johns Hopkins University Press, 1977); on punishment as a cruel relic we should discard see Menninger, *The Crime of Punishment*. In the next chapter we shall consider these and other works expressing such views.

5. *San Francisco Examiner*, August 30, 1988.

should be hurt, as he hurt those who used the drugs he sold. Against those who oppose punishment, or at least punishment that hurts, speak others who say we must punish, and that it must hurt. Punishment is so deeply ingrained in our society that where we expect it but don't have it, we demand justification for its absence. Earlier this century, some anthropologists tried to find out why it was that Eskimos *don't* punish their children—this struck them as demanding an explanation.[6] Legal punishment, too, seems so much a part of us that we demand justification for its absence in cases where we expect it. When the media reported that the twenty-four-year-old son of former vice presidential nominee Geraldine Ferraro was serving his prison sentence for cocaine use in a $1,500-a-month luxury apartment, some were so outraged that the governor of Vermont was pressured to exclude drug offenders from this program of house arrest.[7] The belief is that someone who is rightly condemned deserves to be punished, and failure to punish him is wrong. The state will even nurse an ill inmate on death row so that he will become healthy and capable of receiving the punishment he deserves.[8] Justice demands punishment.

But others call such justice "hypocritical" and see in legal punishment a "morality play."[9] They heed Nietzsche's warning:

> Mistrust all in whom the impulse to punish is powerful. . . . Mistrust all who talk much of their justice! Verily, their souls lack more than honey. And when they call themselves the good and the just, do not forget that they would be pharisees, if only they had—[worldly] power.[10]

6. V. Stefansson, *My Life with the Eskimos*, cited in Elsworth Faris, "The Origin of Punishment," *International Journal of Ethics*, vol. 25, no. 1 (October 1914), pp. 54–67.

7. *New York Times*, September 3, 1988.

8. Robert Nozick notes this in *Philosophical Explanations* (Cambridge, Mass.: Harvard University Press, 1981), p. 370.

9. Menninger, *The Crime of Punishment*, pp. 153–54.

10. Friedrich Nietzsche, *Thus Spoke Zarathustra*, part 2, no. 7; cited in Walter Kaufmann, *Nietzsche* (New York: Random House, 1968), p. 374.

The practice of legal punishment troubles us. It stirs in us
conflicting emotions, and thinking clearly about it is difficult.
One day we may well be persuaded by an editorial protesting
the inhumanity, immorality, and cruelty of inflicting pain, but
perhaps another day a loved one is mugged or raped, and we
scream for revenge. Realizing the cruelty of punishment but
resigned to its necessity, some try to find more humane ways
to punish; enraged by those who would pamper the evil-doer,
and appalled by the devastations of crime, some try to find
more effective ways to punish; whereas others, perhaps convinced that doing harm to another is never just, or does no
good, try to persuade us to abolish the practice.[11]

Still others, not willing to accept the state as "we," view
punishment as coercion by "them" against "us" and question
the justice of any *state* punishment. The January 1989 riots by
blacks in Miami were, in part, an expression by those on the
margin, more "people" than "citizens," of outrage against the
state, and against the society the state represents. These riots,
like Miami's "McDuffy riots" of 1980, were set off when a
police officer, for no apparent reason, shot a black man on a
motorcycle. In the McDuffy riots, violence erupted when the
police officers involved escaped serious punishment; the 1989
riots began immediately after the incident. These riots were
fueled by more than resentment of authority in general. It
mattered to the rioters in 1980 that the police officers who
killed Mr. McDuffy were white, and it mattered to the rioters
in 1989 that the officer involved was Hispanic. A reporter on
the scene of the most recent riots recounts how

> [B]lacks complained that Miami treated blacks unfairly
> and gave favorable treatment to Hispanic immigrants.
> They complained that little was done to help poor blacks,
> many of them lifetime residents here, to find housing and

11. Cf. David Rothman, "Decarcerating Prisoners and Patients,"
in Hyman Gross and Andrew von Hirsch, eds., *Sentencing* (Oxford:
Oxford University Press, 1981). Others who express similar views include Karl Menninger and Randall Barnett, whose work we shall
consider in later chapters.

jobs, but that much was done to help Hispanic immigrants. They pointed to the latest wave of immigrants, Nicaraguans, who are arriving here at the rate of 200 or 300 a day. . . . State Senator Carrie Meek, who is black, said, "As I rode in the Martin Luther King parade, young black people were shouting at me about how they saw Nicaraguans being hired for $5 an hour, and they were yelling, 'Why can't you get me a job?' "[12]

In such circumstances, right, as declared by the laws of the state and enforced by its police, may not seem right to those who are excluded. As one black teenager participating in the 1989 riots shouted to a reporter, "They get everything. Nothing for us."[13] Is it just to punish these people? Does it make any sense to punish them? Aren't they punished enough? Are the laws imposed on them their laws?

Crime is called the cancer of our society; it disrupts our communities and keeps people locked indoors. We erect street barriers because we so fear crime, blocking off whole neighborhoods with huge barrels, or hiring private guards to stand at checkpoints to stop and question strangers.[14] Can we ever realize the republican dream of participatory democracy when we literally build walls between us and our neighbors, when we are too scared to leave our havens and expose ourselves to a public life? Crime is so bad that people are losing faith in the ability of the police to handle violations of the law.

Some not only erect barriers and hire guards, but take justice into their own hands. Recently two men were found not guilty of arson in a case in which they had proudly admitted to the court that they had set a "crack house" (a house frequented by dealers and users of the cocaine-based drug called crack) on fire. They had argued that they acted under duress and in self-defense, that their neighborhood was disintegrating: "Nobody could sit out on the front porch anymore. The

12. *New York Times*, January 18, 1989.
13. Ibid.
14. *New York Times*, December 6, 1988.

kids couldn't play outside." The police would not act, so they took justice into their own hands.[15]

To some, our problem is not that the police lack the manpower or will to punish but, rather, that we must resort to punishment at all; that we must punish reflects a crisis of law and order, a crisis of legitimacy. For example, John Schaar believes that "genuine authority is all but lost to us today." In the "cries of the people who feel that the processes and powers which control their lives are inhuman and destructive," he hears the "outward and visible signs of the underlying crisis of legitimacy in the modern state." In this view, our punishment is pure power, with no authority, and it is authority that we lack, not power. Where authority is lost, "the police can only punish."[16]

Others believe that punishment is not merely symptomatic of, but a reaction to, the crisis of legitimacy. Some Marxist-oriented criminologists argue, for example, that mugging is a constructed crime, created by the state as a reaction to a crisis of hegemony and as part of a war against permissiveness, a war begun in the mid-1960s under the direction of Richard Nixon, who declared "the right of the citizens to walk their own streets, free of the fear of mugging, robbery or rape." In this view, the state—here understood as the courts, police, and media—is said to have constructed a threat, the "crisis of mugging," in order to legitimize an exercise of power that in reality serves only to maintain existing unjust property relations.[17] We need not accept such arguments to see that there is something wrong about us. We are not at ease. Some feel alienated, others downright oppressed. Where authority is lost, the state is a "they," and we are not at home in its practices and institutions.

15. *New York Times*, October 22, 1988, and November 11, 1988.
16. John Schaar, *Legitimacy in the Modern State* (New Brunswick, N.J.: Transaction Books, 1981), pp. 2, 44, 281.
17. Stuart Hall, Chas Critcher, Tony Jefferson, John Clarke, and Brian Roberts, *Policing the Crisis: Mugging, the State, and Law and Order* (London: Macmillan Press, 1978).

We disagree both about the morality of punishing at all and about the legitimacy of state punishment. But we also disagree about numerous issues that arise *inside* the practice of legal punishment. In this book I am concerned not only with the issue of whether the state should punish people at all—is the practice of legal punishment justified?—but also with questions that get raised from within the practice. Given that we do punish, *how* should we punish? For what actions should we punish? Under what circumstances is it appropriate to punish a particular person? Is punishment appropriate if the person did not intend to commit a crime, perhaps because she lacked either the capacity to know the nature and quality of the act she was doing or the capacity of will to conform to the law? Should we punish a person whose guilt was established only by inclusion of evidence obtained illegally? Should we use expedients like plea-bargaining, where we offer a reduced sentence to a defendant in exchange for a plea of guilty, in order to cope with our overburdened courts? Should we put more people into already overcrowded prisons? Should we aim at penal reform by using such practices as parole? Should we sentence certain criminals to die? I shall argue that our conception of why we punish at all provides crucial guidance to us when we assume a position inside the practice, that, in other words, *the justification of the practice as a whole* can guide us in considering *the justification of actions within the practice*. To decide whether to punish someone who is "insane" or who cops a plea, or to execute a convicted murderer, we need to ask whether doing so is consistent with our conception of why we punish at all. In this book I take both an "external" and an "internal" approach to legal punishment; I believe the two approaches are connected. Of course, if we don't think we *should* punish at all, we won't want to assume a position inside the practice.

2. Connecting External and Internal Approaches

There's a difference between on the one hand justifying playing chess, punishing, or giving grades on papers, and on the other hand justifying a particular move, a particular sentence, or a particular grade.[18] Justifying a practice (such as legal punishment) is different from justifying an action within a practice (such as acquitting a defendant shown to be insane). In order to justify—to make good an argument, or show a person or action to be just or right, or defend as right or proper, or give adequate grounds for an action[19]—we need to appeal to some standard of what is right, proper, or just. When we justify an action that is part of a practice, to make our case we can often point to rules of the practice. It's less clear from where standards come in justifying a practice (a point on which I shall elaborate below).

One philosopher, John Rawls, argues that a practice is by definition stipulated by rules,[20] and suggests that from within a practice a practitioner can justify her act *only* by appealing to the rules of the practice: "when the challenge is to the particular action defined by the practice, there is nothing one can do but refer to the rules."[21] But this can't be quite right, since there are practices lacking rules, or with conflicting rules or principles. Of course, lots of practices—especially

18. On the distinction between justifying a practice and justifying an action within a practice, see John Rawls, "Two Concepts of Rules," *Philosophical Review*, vol. 64 (1955), reprinted in Michael Bayles, ed., *Contemporary Utilitarianism* (Gloucester, Mass.: Peter Smith, 1978), from which edition I cite page numbers.

19. *Oxford English Dictionary*.

20. Rawls, "Two Concepts of Rules," p. 88 ("rules define a practice"). Yet Rawls acknowledges that "practice" is an "involved concept" and most likely has "border-line cases" (p. 93).

21. Ibid., p. 91. Rawls does note that there are different sorts of rules: "rules of practices (rules in the strict sense), and maxims and 'rules of thumb'" (p. 93). But he implies that "rules of thumb" don't belong to practices, since practices, by definition, have "rules in the strict sense." On this point I disagree with Rawls: many practices lack "rules in the strict sense."

games or contests—have rules or other clearly acknowledged standards to which we point in order to justify actions we take as participants. In criminal law there are statutes, precedents, sentencing guidelines, and parole board recommendations to which a judge might point to justify a sentencing decision. But some practices have no fixed standards or rules.[22] Take the practice of gift-giving. There's no book in which we can look up how much we should spend (though there are rules of thumb).[23] Lacking rules or clearly acknowledged standards, we might justify an action we've taken within the practice by arguing that it was consistent with our understanding of the point of the practice. Suppose a judge had no rules to guide her in deciding what punishment a convicted felon should receive. Not wanting to be arbitrary, the judge might reflect on the point of the practice of legal punishment to help decide. If she thought the point was to mete out just deserts, she might decide on one sentence; if she thought it was to deter future crimes, she might decide on another. Contrary to Rawls's position that justifications of actions within a practice are given without consideration of the justification of the practice, we *do* sometimes justify our actions by appealing to our understanding of the justification of the practice to which the actions belong.[24]

22. Cf. John Heritage, *Garfinkel and Ethnomethodology* (Cambridge, England: Polity Press, 1984), p. 126: "[F]or vast areas of social conduct, no rules of action at all are formulated or entertained by the participants."

23. There are books on manners with such general guidelines: for example, Letitia Baldridge, *The New Manners for the '90s* (New York: Rawson Associates, 1990). Other practices lacking clearly defined rules include lecturing, grade-giving, and courtesy.

24. Rawls is closer to the truth regarding practices like chess or baseball; in games with fixed rules we don't typically justify actions that are part of the game by appealing to our justification for playing the game at all. (Still, we might; we might want to change the rules of baseball, for instance, by arguing that our proposed rules better serve the purpose of the game.) But with practices like punishment or grade-giving, we typically appeal to the point of the practice.

Even when a practice has rules, sometimes we may think an action that accords with them is nevertheless bad. In such a case, it's hard to argue that the action was not justified, since there are rules to which the actor can point to justify her actions; but sometimes we argue for a change in the rules. We might do this by arguing that the rules in question don't properly serve the purpose of the practice. Sometimes we appeal to the point or purpose of the practice (which, of course, itself might be a matter of interpretation and disagreement) to justify acting against the rules.[25] If a police officer stops a man who is going 5 m.p.h. over the speed limit because he is rushing his wife, who is in labor, to the hospital, the officer will, I would hope, bend the rules. He might justify doing so on the grounds that the point of the practice of giving tickets to speeders is to promote the welfare of the community, and in this case the community's welfare is best served by getting the pregnant woman to the hospital as soon as possible.

There are still other situations in which we might justify an action within a practice that goes against the rules of the practice, but not because we think these rules don't serve the purpose of the practice. Suppose I play chess with a shy, withdrawn child. It might be "bad" for me to make the strategically "right" move, but not according to the rules of chess, or of any other practice (unless we think that kindness is a practice). In making a "wrong" move we step out of the practice—we might say we're no longer really playing chess. We are willing to sacrifice a value internal to chess-playing (winning) for the sake of a conflicting value external to the practice (boosting the confidence of a child).

25. Zimmerman notes how the importance of formal rules is decided by practitioners on a case-by-case basis, in Don Zimmerman, "The Practicalities of Rule Use," in Jack Douglas, ed., *Understanding Everyday Life* (Chicago: Aldine, 1970), p. 225. Harold Garfinkel criticizes the entire model of rules as regulative; he argues that rules don't determine our actions but, rather, provide a "grid" "by reference to which *whatever* is done will become visible and assessable" (Heritage, *Garfinkel and Ethnomethodology*, p. 117; cf. pp. 120, 126, 128).

Practitioners, in justifying actions within a practice, can (though they need not) appeal to the practice's standards or rules, if it has any, or to an interpretation of the point of the practice as a whole or of the principle(s) immanent in it. One way we know we are engaged in a practice is that there are such features, either rules or a point, to which we can appeal to justify our actions.

But what happens when we justify the whole practice? Practitioners don't often engage in this activity. Someone playing chess justifies her moves by pointing to the rules and strategies of the game. When challenged, she might justify playing chess ("because it's challenging," "it sharpens the mind," "it's an outlet for my suppressed anger"), but making such challenges is not part of the practice of playing chess, is not something the practitioners—the chess players—are likely to do. If a challenge is made, the context in which it arises will determine what counts as a good answer. Consider: "Why are you playing chess instead of doing your homework?" "Because I like playing chess better." Or, "Why are you playing chess instead of checkers?" "Because checkers is mostly luck, chess is mostly skill." Here the context determines in part the reason given. But it would be strange to consider, abstracting from all particular contexts in which such a question could arise, what the justification is of playing chess. Maybe because it's fun, or because it develops the mind. Why not? What would count as a satisfactory answer? Unlike the cases in which we justify actions that are part of a practice, in cases in which we justify the practice as a whole there are no clear standards to which we can point.[26]

We rarely, if ever, justify the practice of chess. It takes some imagination to think of a context in which doing so would make sense (perhaps I am at a toy store thinking of which

26. In chapter five, section 2, I elaborate on this point by arguing that social practices lack fixed grounds, or "foundational" justifications. In justifying practices we can give only reasons that persuade, perhaps by appealing to a system of shared convictions: justifications of practices ultimately are "nonfoundational."

game to buy, or my daughter wants to dedicate her life to chess-playing instead of becoming a lawyer, so I ask, "Why chess?"). But for other practices, legal punishment included, we have no problem making sense of the question "Why do it?" and much depends on our arriving at a satisfactory answer.[27] I shall argue that to know how we should go about determining the guilt of a defendant or the sentence for a convicted person, we need to know what the point of punishing is—we need a convincing answer to the question "Why punish?" Practitioners don't often ask the question, yet they determine guilt, sentence, lock up, and do all the other things that are part of legal punishment. But, as we shall see, many of us don't accept what is done, and think it should be done differently. We see a dire need to step outside the practice in order to find a convincing account of its purpose, so that we can come back inside and guide practitioners. But when appealing to a justification for the practice as a whole, we must keep in mind that there are no obvious guidelines for judging what's the "right" justification. Perhaps there are more than one.

3. Immanent Criticism

The theorist who steps outside the practice in order to think about it becomes an *immanent critic* when she uses her account of the purpose of the practice to criticize actions in actual practice that diverge from this purpose.[28] Immanent criticism is possible because it is possible for us to have ideals

27. To name a few others: slavery, marriage, promising, torture, war, professional boxing, grade-giving.
28. On the idea of the critic invoking her society's own shared values as the grounds of criticism, see Hanna Pitkin, *The Concept of Representation* (Berkeley: University of California Press, 1967); and *Wittgenstein and Justice* (Berkeley: University of California Press, 1972); Michael Walzer, *Interpretation and Social Criticism* (Cambridge, Mass.: Harvard University Press, 1987); and Steven B. Smith, *Hegel's Critique of Liberalism* (Chicago: University of Chicago Press, 1989), pp. 10, 13, 169–75.

that in principle guide us, but for us occasionally (or even often) to act against those ideals. Actuality, or a practice as it is actually carried out, can diverge from the practice as it would be if it were consistently carried out according to its ideals.[29] Of course, if the actual practice almost never accords with those ideals, we shall have to wonder whether we have gotten those ideals right.

The standards the immanent critic uses to judge actual practices are immanent in the practices. The immanent critic answers the question "How ought we to punish?" by appealing, not to some abstract or transcendental standard, but to how we *do* punish, finding implicit principles that on the whole make sense of the practice. By adopting the strategy of immanent criticism, the theorist gains distance from, yet remains connected to the actual world. The immanent critic works from within our practices, criticizing them according to standards she finds already present. I believe that the greatest advantage of immanent criticism as a theoretical strategy is precisely this reliance, not on transcendent visions, but on the materials at hand.

4. Punishing for Justice: A Retributive Immanent Criticism of Legal Punishment

In turning to the practice of legal punishment, we shall see that there are two very persuasive accounts of the purpose of,

29. The general idea of abstracting from a practice its essential purpose or idea and taking this theory of the practice as both a justification for it and a standard by which to criticize it was nicely articulated by Hanna Pitkin: "For whatever reasons, and with no deliberate, common purpose, men may gradually develop fixed ways of doing something—institutionalized behavior which has become habitual. From this patterned behavior they may begin to abstract express ideas about what it is for, how it is to be done, what principles and purposes underlie it. And, in due time, those principles may themselves come to be used as new aims for revising the institution, as critical standards for assessing the way in which it functions and improving it" (Pitkin, *The Concept of Representation*, p. 236; cf. Pitkin, *Wittgenstein and Justice*, pp. 186–92).

and the principle immanent in, the practice. In chapter three we shall see how the *utilitarian* believes that we punish to deter future crime, or incapacitate the dangerous criminal, or perhaps reform him, but, in any case, that we punish for some future good, or to augment social utility, and that in punishing we are, and should be, guided by the principle that we should augment pleasure and decrease pain;[30] whereas the *retributivist* believes that we punish to mete out justice, express society's righteous anger and condemnation, and vindicate right, and that in punishing we are, and should be, guided by the principle that we should punish only when doing so serves justice and right.[31] In chapter four we shall see how the disagreement over why we punish at all matters practically. We take an internal approach, examining conflicting utilitarian and retributive resolutions to problems that emerge from inside the practice. There we shall see also that the problems practitioners face are not neatly resolved merely by commitment to one or another conception—utilitarian or retributive—of why we punish at all; we hold to values outside the practice that conflict with values internal to it, and these other values must also be taken into account in thinking about some of the problems of legal punishment.

In this book I defend a specific version of retributivism. I shall argue that though legal punishment has many beneficial consequences, we should not confuse these consequences with the practice's purpose, which is to mete out justice and vindicate right. I am persuaded by Hegel's point, that

> [d]eterrence and reform are important goals [of punishment], and one should ask what reforms or level of deterrence society demands. But another question is what justice demands, and every human being feels this difference.[32]

30. This is a very general account. Not all utilitarian theories use the measurements "pleasure" and "pain"; we shall be more precise when we discuss utilitarian theories in chapter 3.

31. There are various accounts of what retribution means, and in chapter 3 we shall spend considerable time distinguishing them.

32. G. W. F. Hegel, *Vorlesungen über Rechtsphilosophie* (1818–

I shall argue that on the whole the retributivist gives a better, more complete account of why we punish, and therefore of the principle that does and should guide us within the practice. There are at least two formidable difficulties with the position I defend, that of retributivist immanent criticism, and much of our time shall be spent grappling with them. The first problem is faced by *any* immanent critic of *any* practice. The immanent critic steps outside the practice to reflect on its purpose, in order to come back inside to justify and criticize actions within the practice by appealing to the practice's purpose. But sometimes we will not want to come back inside our practices. Some of our practices may be bad root and branch, and we won't regard any of its actions as justified. Sometimes we need a radical vision that challenges our commitment to our practices, and such a vision the immanent critic cannot offer. The critical force of *immanent* criticism is purchased at the cost of giving up *radical* criticism. Whether this cost is too great depends on whether or not we can be reconciled to our practices. The immanent critic believes that we can persevere with our ideals even in the face of a nonideal practice, if we bring the actual practice back into line with its ideals, or perhaps with an adjusted account of those ideals. But the radical critic rejects those ideals and any adjusted account. I address this problem in chapter two, where I consider the radical criticisms of legal punishment offered by Nietzsche, Foucault, Karl Menninger, and Marxists.

A second problem with retributivist immanent criticism of legal punishment is a problem inherent not in immanent criticism in general, but in immanent criticism of practices whose purposes are "essentially contested."[33] I shall consider the argument that the retributivist accounts for so many of the fea-

---

1831), 4 vols., ed. Karl-Heinz Ilting (Stuttgart-Bad Cannstatt: Friedrich Fromann, 1973), vol. 4, p. 286.

33. A practice is essentially contested if our disagreement about its purpose and meaning is built into the practice—that is, if contestation is an essential feature of the practice. In chapter 5 I give a more detailed account of what it means to say that a practice is essentially contested.

tures of our practice of legal punishment that consistently to violate the retributivist ideal, perhaps by punishing people who do not deserve our condemnation, would be to engage, not in punishment, but in some other practice.[34] But I shall suggest that this argument, although consistent with the retributivist position I defend, ignores what I think is a truth about legal punishment. In chapter five I shall argue that legal punishment is an essentially contested practice; conflicting principles are immanent in and essential to legal punishment. It's unconvincing to claim that to punish in violation of the retributivist ideal is not really to "punish." In chapter five we shall consider how the immanent critic, whose strategy is to use the principle(s) immanent in a practice to justify or criticize actions taken within the practice, is to cope with a practice that is essentially contested, that has conflicting principles immanent in it—in other words, how we can be committed to the position that we punish for justice, while acknowledging that legal punishment is essentially contested. I believe that the retributive account which I shall defend is stronger for acknowledging that legal punishment contains conflicting values. Acknowledging this fact forces the retributivist to adjust his conception of the ideals of punishment. This needn't mean giving up his commitment to retribution, but it is likely to result in an account more persuasive to those who share in the practice.

34. Rawls, in "Two Concepts of Rules," uses the term "telishment" to describe such a practice.

2

Radical Criticisms of the Practice of Legal Punishment

1. Radical Criticism

There are advantages to being connected, to accepting the materials at hand. We can't just go and start a society from scratch. That a practice already exists is not, however, in itself a justification for that practice. Lots of objectionable practices have existed and still do exist—slavery, infanticide, witch-burning, hazing, human sacrifice, and cannibalism, to name but a few. Still, that we share a practice, and have all sorts of expectations and commitments because we have this practice, is one reason to continue with it. How much stronger a reason we need depends on the strength of the challenge made to the practice.

Those who stand inside the practice to justify certain actions or to criticize others, by appealing either to the rules of the practice or to an interpretation of the practice's purpose or justification, by virtue of their position inside the practice are committed to that practice and at least in this sense presuppose its justification. (The immanent critic I described in chapter one is such a person.) Perhaps the person inside the practice has never considered a challenge to the practice as a whole; perhaps if she did, she might come to the conclusion that the practice as a whole is not justified. But until that challenge is made, the practitioner just "practices," for the tasks at hand would never get done if she often paused to reflect on whether it is a good thing that we have the practice at all.

In this chapter we shall consider arguments by those who are not committed to the practice of legal punishment. They are outsiders and have little to say directly to the practitioner who is concerned with whether the practice requires acting in this way or that. The radical critic in effect denies that there can be a sufficient justification for any action that is part of the practice; she concludes that the whole practice, root and branch, serves no good purpose, or perhaps a malign one. In contrast, the immanent critic might reject particular justifications that are given within the practice but accepts that in principle actions within the practice can be justified.[1] The immanent critic might thus object to a particular criminal-law doctrine on the grounds that it goes against the principles underlying and justifying the practice as a whole; he might, for example, challenge the particular verdict of a jury. The theorist who assumes the role of immanent critic is, then, situated inside the practice.

Of course the theorist needn't be literally engaged in the practice. A philosopher or theorist can think about the sorts of problems facing such actual practitioners as legislators, lawyers, judges, sentencing commission members, and police officers. She can imagine herself in the position of an actual

---

1. In his *Law's Empire* (Cambridge, Mass.: Harvard University Press, 1986), pp. 78–83, Ronald Dworkin distinguishes three sorts of skepticism: internal, global internal, and external. The radical critics I consider in this chapter are like what Dworkin calls global internal skeptics. Dworkin's external skeptic denies the possibility of justifying a practice, perhaps for metaphysical reasons. In this work I am not interested in such skeptics (although perhaps Nietzsche is one, though not for metaphysical reasons). What I call an immanent critic is like Dworkin's internal skeptic: Dworkin says the internal skeptic objects to our claims and against him we give reasons and claim to be right.

practitioner and give a justification that could be used in practice. Most of the radical critics we shall consider in this chapter don't do this.[2] They are skeptical of the whole practice and offer no advice to those committed to the practice and needing guidance about how to proceed. In this chapter we look at radical criticisms, and in chapters three and four we shall look at immanent criticisms, so that we can judge for ourselves the advantages and disadvantages of the two sorts of criticism.

Although it is difficult to categorize neatly the radical critics we shall consider, the following division is convenient: "genealogists" explain the origins of punishment; "functionalists," some of whom are also genealogists, explain the function legal punishment serves; and "Marxists," or radical criminologists, also genealogists of a sort, explain legal punishment in a capitalist society as a practice reflecting the class structure of that society. In all cases, the radical critic provides an understanding (of the origin or function) of punishment that is intended to raise our consciousness, to get us to see that really we are not at home in this practice.

2. Genealogist as Radical Critic: Nietzsche and Foucault

A genealogy is an account of an individual's descent from an ancestor; thus, a genealogy of a practice intends to show the origins of the practice. The genealogist tells us why, historically, we have our practices. What we have to explore is how the understanding given to us by the genealogist might help us cope with our practices. The work of Friedrich Nietzsche and Michel Foucault will serve as our paradigms of genealogy as radical criticism.

2. The one exception is Karl Menninger. As we shall soon see, Menninger hedges. Sometimes he argues that we should not punish. But sometimes he accepts that we have the practice and proceeds to give advice on its details—for example, that we should use psychiatric and medical expertise in determining sentencing.

2.1 Nietzsche

Nietzsche does not discuss the practice of legal punishment systematically.[3] The only extensive source for his views on the subject is his second essay in *On the Genealogy of Morals*, although his other works contain several passages addressing punishment. The tone of all of these sources is critical. But before we judge their force, let us see their substance.

Retributivists often argue that the essence of punishment is the just deserts it metes out to the guilty. Nietzsche argues that punishment did not arise from an initial judgment that the criminal deserves punishment—this is "in fact an extremely late and subtle form of human judgment and inference." The origin of punishment is more primitive:

> Throughout the greater part of human history punishment was not imposed because one held the wrongdoer responsible for his deed, thus not on the presupposition that only the guilty one should be punished: rather, as parents still punish their children, from anger at some harm or injury, vented on the one who caused it—but this anger is held in check and modified by the idea that every injury has its equivalent and can actually be paid back, even if only through the pain of the culprit. And whence did this primeval, deeply rooted, perhaps by now ineradicable idea draw its power—this idea of an equivalence between injury and pain? . . . in the contractual relationship between creditor and debtor, which is as old as the idea of "legal subjects" and in turn points back to the fundamental forms of buying, selling, barter, trade, and traffic.[4]

3. He doesn't discuss *anything* systematically. Moreover, Nietzsche's interest in punishment may be limited to its being a convenient example for his more general point about the construction of meaning.

4. Friedrich Nietzsche, *On the Genealogy of Morals* and *Ecce Homo*, trans. Walter Kaufmann and R. J. Hollingdale (New York: Vintage, 1969), essay 2, section 4. In citing Nietzsche, I refer to essay and section numbers.

Punishment emerged as a "right of the masters"—the credi-
tors—to "experience for once the exalted sensation of being
allowed to despise and mistreat someone as 'beneath him' "—
punishment was "a warrant for and title to cruelty."[5] Before
Christian *ressentiment* transvalued the power of the masters
from something "good" to something "evil," teaching man to
"be ashamed of all his instincts," cruelty was essential to a
"cheerful" life.[6] In the days when we did not repress our instincts, we reveled in and celebrated cruelty: "[W]ithout cruelty there is no festival: thus the longest and most ancient part
of human history teaches—and in punishment there is so much
that is festive!"[7]

Nietzsche thinks that punishment as now practiced is no
longer as it originally was. For if punishment still embodied
the strength of the powerful who punished, we would, he suggests, no longer punish:

> The "creditor" always becomes more humane to the ex-
> tent that he has grown richer. . . . It is not unthinkable
> that a society might attain such a consciousness of power
> that it could allow itself the noblest luxury possible to
> it—letting those who harm it go unpunished. "What are
> my parasites to me?" it might say. "May they live and
> prosper: I am strong enough for that!"[8]

Punishment arose as the expression of the will of the powerful.
But a reversal has taken place. To be powerful in primitive
days was to be cruel and cheerful;[9] to be powerful in modern
times is to be able to resist being cruel, to resist punishing.
To punish is no longer a sign of power; the power that now
punishes is too weak to be able not to punish.

5. Ibid., essay 2, section 6.
6. Ibid., essay 2, section 7. For the meaning of *ressentiment* and
its importance to Nietzsche's account of punishment, see Walter
Kaufmann, *Nietzsche* (New York: Random House, 1968), pp. 371–78.
7. Nietzsche, *Genealogy*, essay 2, section 6.
8. Ibid., essay 2, section 10.
9. Primitive=prehistoric: ibid., essay 2, section 9.

Ressentiment changes both who punishes and what punishment is. The power that now punishes understands punishment to be a means of upholding justice by meting out retribution, or of treating the sick, or of preventing crime. Nietzsche claims that our present understanding of punishment belies its origins:

> Thus one also imagined that punishment was devised for punishing. But purposes and utilities are only signs that a will to power has become master of something less powerful and imposed upon it the character of a function.[10]

Nietzsche is telling us in this passage that the institution of punishment—the remnant of the "will to power"—now masters the weak, not they it, and dictates to them the necessity of seeking retribution or doing what has utility. The weak don't make up their own institution, but receive the old, which, with new managers, takes on a meaning that belies the original.

Nietzsche, I believe, wants us to see a great irony about punishment. The original will to punish was not a will to revenge or to seek retribution; it was "the will of life,"[11] the will of the powerful masters who reveled in cruelty. The will to revenge that now punishes, that has occupied the institution left behind by the will to power, is the will of the weak, the will of *ressentiment*; it is what has emerged as part of the sinister "European culture" with its spreading morality of pity, a morality that has "seized even on philosophers and made them ill." The will to revenge is the will of the nihilist;[12] it is a will counter to the will of life. The present power that punishes is the vengeful tarantula, which hangs its webs, but is really frail: "[T]ouch it, that it tremble!"[13]

10. Ibid., essay 2, section 12.
11. Ibid., essay 2, section 11.
12. Ibid., Preface, section 5.
13. Friedrich Nietzsche, *Thus Spoke Zarathustra*, trans. Walter Kaufmann (New York: Penguin, 1978), "On the Tarantulas."

What conclusions does Nietzsche draw from his genealogy of punishment? He makes several suggestions. He suggests that retributive punishment—the punishment of the weak that seeks justice—will be ineffective, perhaps because the new appropriators of punishment are wielding a weapon effective only in the hands of those capable of using it. The instrument of punishment was appropriate to its original users, who festively enjoyed their tool. But in the hands of its new managers, punishment is put to new uses for which it is ill suited (for example, to make the criminal repent):

> It is precisely among criminals and convicts that the sting of conscience is extremely rare; prisons and penitentiaries are not the kind of hotbed in which this species of gnawing worm [men of conscience who repent] is likely to flourish. . . . If we consider those millennia before the history of man, we may unhesitatingly assert that it was precisely through punishment that the development of the feeling of guilt was most powerfully hindered.[14]

Nietzsche says it would be a relief to be free of the idea of sin and punishment, which is part of the "old [though not prehistoric] instinct of revenge."[15] We should rise above this practice of the weak, of the Nay-sayers:

> Let us stop thinking so much about punishment, reproaching, and improving others. . . . Let us not contend in a direct fight—and that is what all reproaching, punishing, and attempts to improve others amount to. Let us rather raise ourselves that much higher. . . . No, let us not become darker ourselves on their account, like all those who punish others and feel dissatisfied. Let us sooner step aside. Let us look away.[16]

14. Nietzsche, *Genealogy*, essay 2, section 14.
15. Friedrich Nietzsche, *Morgenröte* (Stuttgart: Alfred Kröner, 1964), section 202.
16. Friedrich Nietzsche, *The Gay Science*, trans. Walter Kaufmann (New York: Random House, 1974), section 321.

> I do not want to wage war against what is ugly. I do not
> want to accuse; I do not even want to accuse those who
> accuse. Looking away shall be my only negation. And all
> in all and on the whole: some day I wish to be only a
> Yes-sayer.[17]

To the modern power that punishes, that weak, venomous,
vengeful spider or snake, Nietzsche says: "But take back your
poison. You are not rich enough to give it to me."[18]

Nietzsche is critical of punishment, but is he critical only
of punishment as it has become—of the perverted form of
punishment that is our own practice? Sometimes Nietzsche
appears to be calling us back to our original home, to a pre-
historic practice of punishment that in its cruelty is "festive"
and celebratory of the greatness of the strong. In this view,
Nietzsche is saying that the meaning of punishment has
changed, it has become a sickly and spiteful institution of revenge, a weapon of the weak in their reaction against the
strong; and Nietzsche is pointing us back to our original or
natural instinct to dominate, beckoning us to express our natural will to life. Although there are passages to support such
a reading,[19] I think this view misses Nietzsche's more potent
point, and the essentially critical, not constructive, character
of his project.

Nietzsche insists that the origins of a practice or institution
do not tell us its purpose or value:

> the cause of the origin of a thing and its eventual utility,
> its actual employment and place in a system of purposes,

17. Ibid., section 276.
18. *Thus Spoke Zarathustra*, "On the Adder's Bite." There
Nietzsche also writes, "It is nobler to declare oneself wrong than to
insist on being right—especially when one is right." And in the section
"On the Tarantulas": "For that man be delivered from revenge, that
is for me the bridge to the highest hope, and a rainbow after long
storms." Also, *Ecce Homo* (essay 1, section 5): "not to take the punishment upon oneself but the guilt would be divine."
19. For example, the tone of essay 1, section 11, in the *Genealogy*,
challenging the morality of *ressentiment* and praising the beast man
over the maggot men.

lie worlds apart; whatever exists, having somehow come into being, is again and again reinterpreted to new ends, taken over, transformed, and redirected by some power superior to it. . . . However well one has understood the utility of any physiological organ (or of a legal institution, a social custom, a political usage, a form in art or in a religious cult), this means nothing regarding its origin: however uncomfortable and disagreeable this may sound to older ears—for one had always believed that to understand the demonstrable purpose, the utility of a thing, a form, or an institution, was also to understand the reason why it originated—the eye being made for seeing, the hand being made for grasping.[20]

Nietzsche warns us against mistakenly thinking that our conception of the value of a practice accounts for the origins of the practice. Nietzsche's view in the *Genealogy* is, rather, that practices and institutions first emerge in history and subsequently come to assume various meanings: we invent purposes for them, we interpret their meanings.[21] Nietzsche is aware that "punishment" means different things, and he lists several: punishment can mean to render harmless, to recompense, to prevent future disturbances, to inspire fear, to repay, to purify; it can refer to a festive rape and mockery of an enemy, or a declaration of war.[22] Nietzsche's point is that none of these, alone, is the true meaning or purpose of punishment:

[T]he concept "punishment" possesses in fact not one meaning but a whole synthesis of "meanings": the previous history of punishment in general, the history of its employment for the most various purposes, finally crystallizes into a kind of unity that is hard to disentangle, hard to analyze and, as must be emphasized, totally indefinable. (Today it is impossible to say for certain why people are really punished: all concepts in which an en-

20. *Genealogy*, essay 2, section 12.
21. Ibid., essay 2, section 13.
22. Ibid.

tire process is semiotically concentrated elude definition; only that which has no history is definable.)[23]

At certain times one element "appears to overcome all the remaining elements" and mark the true meaning of punishment.[24] But Nietzsche says this is only an appearance; there is no essence of punishment, even though we can speak of punishment as one practice, as a "unity."[25]

Nietzsche's genealogy, then, seems directed, not at calling us back to the true purpose and meaning of punishment, but at challenging all claims to know its true meaning. He attacks retributivists, who see justice as the essence of punishment; he attacks utilitarians, who see deterrence as the essence of punishment.[26] The value of genealogy lies, not in telling us the true purpose of punishment, but in helping us see that there is no true purpose.

There is much that is attractive in Nietzsche's view. In chapter five I shall embrace Nietzsche's *nonfoundationalism*, his view that the justification of a practice depends essentially on our interpretation of the practice, and that no one interpretation can claim to articulate the true meaning of the practice. But there is also much that is disquieting. Is Nietzsche, like the Socrates he portrayed in his earlier *The Birth of Tragedy*, a "theoretic man" who delights in unmasking and who "finds the highest object of pleasure in the process of an ever happy uncovering?"[27] More to our point than deciding Nietzsche's

23. Ibid.
24. Ibid.
25. Cf. Michel Foucault's account of Nietzsche's genealogy, in *Language, Counter-Memory, Practice*, ed. Donald Bouchard (Ithaca: Cornell University Press, 1977), p. 142: "[I]f the genealogist listens to history, he finds that behind things there is not a timeless and essential secret, but the secret that they have no essence or that their essence was fabricated in a piecemeal fashion. . . . Examining the history of reason, he learns that it was born in an altogether 'reasonable' fashion—from chance."
26. Deterrence is his example of what at one time "appears" to be the true purpose of punishment (*Genealogy*, essay 2, section 13).
27. Friedrich Nietzsche, *The Birth of Tragedy*, trans. Walter Kaufmann (New York: Vintage, 1967), p. 94.

own intentions, does Nietzsche, who seems to challenge the validity of every justification of the practice of legal punishment, offer practical criticism? Does his account better equip us to live with our practices, perhaps to reform them? It is not easy to see how. Nietzsche clearly is not engaged in the activity of justifying actions within the practice. But it's not clear that he intends even to engage in the activity of justifying (or denying the justification of) the whole practice; and his account is not obviously intended to move us to abolish our practice. Sometimes Nietzsche seems to assume a position of radical skepticism that claims there can be no justifications.[28] Whatever Nietzsche's intentions are, it is difficult to see how Nietzsche's account is in any sense practical, or useful to the practitioner committed to the criminal justice system.

Toward the end of the second essay in the *Genealogy*, Nietzsche asks himself: "What are you really doing, erecting an ideal or knocking one down?" He answers:

> But have you ever asked yourselves sufficiently how much the erection of *every* ideal on earth has cost? How much reality has had to be misunderstood and slandered, how many lies have had to be sanctified, how many consciences disturbed, how much "God" sacrificed every time? If a temple is to be erected *a temple must be destroyed*: that is the law—let anyone who can show me a case in which it is not fulfilled.[29]

The immanent critic, committed to our practices, would respond: If we destroy the temple that houses us, we will be homeless. I think this is a powerful objection to Nietzsche's project of radical criticism. Of course, it is the immanent critic's burden to persuade us that the home we have is better than none or than one we might build from scratch.

28. In this view Nietzsche is what Dworkin calls an external skeptic: see chapter 2, note 1.
29. *Genealogy*, essay 2, section 24, Nietzsche's emphasis.

2.2 *Foucault*

Foucault's account of punishment has its most complete expression in *Discipline and Punish*.[30] His thesis in this work is that the Enlightenment penal system that emerged in the late eighteenth and early nineteenth centuries, though on its surface marking a reaction to the old system of equating punishment with pain and torture and spectacle, in fact is but a new mask for what was and is essentially a politics of power.[31] Although the Enlightenment penal system denies that it acts inhumanely, its imposition of a bureaucratic structure of psychologists and parole boards upon the penal process serves only to distance the judge from the actual act of punishment.[32] Punishment is made to appear more humane—it is said to be a cure[33]—but in fact it is even more devious: it is intended no longer to punish the offense, but to supervise the individual.[34] In the new system we no longer torture the body. Instead we deprive the offender of some liberty, often by placing him in a house of correction for treatment; but in Foucault's view there is no such thing as a non-corporal punishment, for depriving the body of its rights is the same as inflicting pain.[35]

Foucault presents his account as genealogy. He offers an explanation of the transition from the old to the new system of punishment. In the old system the power to punish was held exclusively by the sovereign,[36] and punishment was a public spectacle that "displayed for all to see the power relation that gave his force to the law."[37] In the new system, the power relation in punishment remains but no longer displays itself publicly.[38] Punishment now takes place behind closed doors,

    30. Michel Foucault, *Discipline and Punish: The Birth of the Prison*, trans. Alan Sheridan (1975; reprinted New York: Vintage, 1979).
    31. Ibid., p. 55.
    32. Ibid., p. 13.
    33. Ibid., pp. 16–17, 22, 101.
    34. Ibid., p. 18.
    35. Ibid., pp. 16, 101.
    36. Ibid., p. 35.
    37. Ibid., p. 50.
    38. Cf. ibid., p. 55.

hence the birth of the prison and houses of correction. Why the change? Foucault sees as causal, not a new spirit of Enlightenment ideals, but shifting mechanisms or tactics of power. There was a "closer penal mapping of the social body."[39]

> Ultimately, what one is trying to restore in this technique of correction is . . . the obedient subject, the individual subjected to habits, rules, orders, an authority that is exercised continually around him and upon him. . . . The agent of punishment must exercise a total power, which no third party can disturb; the individual to be corrected must be entirely enveloped in the power that is being exercised over him.[40]

Foucault explains punishment as a "political tactic"; it is a practice "based on the principle of the technology of power."[41] To understand punishment we must study "political anatomy."[42]

Punishment is just one manifestation, to Foucault, of what he sees as power:

> Punishment is a functioning of a power that is exercised on those punished, and more generally on those being supervised, on madmen, children, those stuck at a machine, etc.[43]

The underlying process of power reveals itself not only in punishment but in the concern for and control over detail, and in various techniques of domination.[44] Other manifestations of this power include the discipline of factories, schools, barracks, and hospitals.[45] Even the keeping of clinical records

39. Ibid., pp. 77–78.
40. Ibid., pp. 128–29.
41. Ibid., pp. 23–24.
42. Ibid., p. 28.
43. Ibid., p. 29.
44. Ibid., p. 141.
45. Ibid., pp. 227–28.

of an individual's medical facts represents, to Foucault, a power's "coercion over bodies."[46]

The underlying process of power also sets up masks or myths to hide its ugly workings. One of the myths is the "logical nexus" linking punishment to crime. Foucault argues that the politics of power makes punishment a sign for crime and understood to go together with crime: society links crime and punishment via signs,[47] and by this linkage it conceals the power that actually punishes.[48] In another essay Foucault speaks of "rights" as a mask: theories of rights serve to efface the domination intrinsic to power, in order to make power appear as legitimate, as something we are legally obligated to obey.[49]

Power, then, is what for Foucault accounts for the development of the practice of legal punishment. Power is an "underlying force." The penal process reflects invisible, "more profound processes."[50] Foucault says this underlying process of power is so profound that it constitutes our concept of truth: "There is no knowledge that does not presuppose and constitute at the same time power relations."[51]

The underlying process of power is invisible, like Marx's mole. There are similarities between Foucault's explanation and that of many Marxists, and Foucault is sympathetic to some of the Marxists we shall take up.[52] But Foucault says he rejects simple class analyses.[53] In another essay he breaks with the Marxists in not seeing power as the domination of one

46. Ibid., p. 191.
47. Ibid., pp. 104–5, 109.
48. Ibid., p. 105.
49. Michel Foucault, *Power/Knowledge*, ed. Colin Gordon (Suffolk: Harvester Press, 1980), p. 95.
50. Foucault, *Discipline and Punish*, p. 210. Cf. p. 139: "[B]eneath every set of figures, we must seek not a meaning, but a precaution; we must situate them not only in the inextricability of a functioning, but in the coherence of a tactic."
51. Ibid., p. 27.
52. Cf. ibid., pp. 24–25, on the work of Rusche/Kirchheimer; also pp. 273–75, on the class basis of punishment.
53. Ibid., pp. 24–25, 54.

group or class over another. Rather, "power must be analysed as something which circulates, or rather as something which only functions in the form of a chain."[54] For Marx, power is a possession: it may be held, transferred, or alienated. For Foucault, power has the character of a network; its threads extend everywhere. Power or domination can't be terminated merely by overthrowing a regime.[55] Foucault rejects the particular Marxist explanation of punishment, which we shall discuss later in this chapter, but not the Marxists' general project of explaining punishment. Foucault explains punishment as historically and at present the result of the functioning of a power.

The power to which Foucault refers may strike us as ineffable, even after reading the concrete accounts in *Discipline and Punish* and elsewhere.[56] What are we to make of Foucault's account: is it persuasive? is it in any sense practical?

First, is Foucault's explanation persuasive? There is certainly something compelling in Foucault's vision: he directs us to look again at familiar institutions—schools, hospitals, factories, prisons, armies—and see in them something we might have missed before. Foucault is persuasive in showing how all of these institutions discipline and normalize us.[57] Per-

---

54. Foucault, *Power/Knowledge*, p. 98.

55. See Barry Smart, *Foucault, Marxism and Critique* (London: Routledge and Kegan Paul, 1983), pp. 81–87.

56. The power Foucault describes is not always ineffable. In the book he edited, *I, Pierre Rivière* (New York: Penguin, 1975), Foucault interprets the penal process that led to the eventual conviction and incarceration of the parricide Pierre Rivière as a struggle of powers. The documents of the trial and Pierre's own memoir of his deed are seen by Foucault as narratives that became facts, part of a history "below the level of power" (205–6). Concretely, this means, for example, that the testimony regarding Pierre's sanity given at the trial by various medical experts reflected a power struggle within the medical and psychological fields and also between the fields of law and medicine.

57. The English verb "to discipline," with its dual meaning of "to punish" and "to make regular or obedient," is particularly well suited for Foucault's argument.

haps, now, we will see our world differently, in a new light. But what precisely is it that Foucault wants us to see?

Foucault argues that if we look at the organization of our institutions we shall see there the urge to discipline and impress power upon individuals—we shall see "coercion."[58] But is this the best interpretation of what we see? Many institutions have aims the achievement of which requires order. In a symphony orchestra or a chamber group each member must count strictly, under the gaze of each other or of the conductor. Is this a sign of power at work? Is the discipline in the orchestra or chamber group evidence of an urge to control the body? Why is it bad to be watched or observed?[59] Isn't it sometimes good? Can't it show that someone loves or cares about us? Which judgment of the gaze is best: that it reveals coercive designs, or loving care? Is Foucault's interpretation of the keeping of clinical records as "coercion over bodies" the best account of this practice? Foucault also says that the isolation of contagious patients is a technique of discipline, a tactic of power.[60] Is this the best account of why doctors decide to isolate certain patients?[61]

In advancing his own interpretation of legal punishment, Foucault challenges past and present justifiers of the practice, in effect arguing that we cannot take them at their word when they offer their justifications. Although the Enlightenment re-

58. Foucault, *Discipline and Punish*, p. 169.
59. See Foucault's discussion of Bentham's Panopticon: ibid., ch. 7.
60. Ibid., p. 144.
61. Norman Jacobson has suggested to me that we might understand Foucault's theorizing about discipline and the coercive ways society normalizes us as part of his personal struggle to engage us in his plight as a homosexual in a society that regards homosexuality as abnormal. This might make us more sympathetic to Foucault's account, but I'm not sure it makes more convincing his interpretations of particular practices such as legal punishment or the isolation of contagious patients. Also, Dennis McEnnerney has suggested to me, in defense of Foucault, that Foucault's account of the keeping of clinical records might be a convincing interpretation of the practice in Foucault's France, if not of the practice elsewhere.

formers gave their reasons for changing the practice of punishment, Foucault imputes to them a different motive from the one they professed. "The true objective" of the reform movement, he says, was to set up a new economy of the power to punish, and not, as Enlightenment reformers claimed, to establish the right to punish on equitable principles.[62] The justification for reform, in Foucault's view, was really to "insert the power to punish more deeply into the social body."[63]

> [To] constitute a new economy and a new technology of the power to punish: these are no doubt the essential *raisons d'être* of penal reform in the 18th century.[64]

Foucault repeatedly devalues the role in reform, and perhaps challenges the sincerity, of Enlightenment ideals of humanity.[65] At one point Foucault suggests that Enlightenment thinkers and juristic reformers collaborated (unknowingly?) with "technicians of power":

> While jurists or philosophers were seeking in the pact [social contract] a primal model for the construction or reconstruction of the social body, the soldiers and with them the technicians of discipline were elaborating procedures for the individual and collective coercion of bodies.[66]

Other times, Foucault indicates that his argument is not about the desire for power: his is an argument about institutions, structural features, and their relation to technology.[67] Ultimately Foucault's argument depends on the persuasiveness of his account of our institutions and practices, and to be persuasive he has to convince us that the justifications given in practice can't be accepted at face value. Yet Foucault seems

62. Foucault, *Discipline and Punish*, p. 80.
63. Ibid., p. 82.
64. Ibid., p. 89.
65. Ibid., pp. 74–75, 78–79, 81–82, 303.
66. Ibid., p. 169.
67. Cf. ibid., p. 163 (the discussion about the rifle).

unwilling even to engage in dialogue with Enlightenment reformers, of whose intentions he is suspicious—but what if these
reformers were sincere?

Even if we were persuaded by Foucault's interpretation of
legal punishment, the question would still remain: How does
Foucault's theory bear on our practice? Foucault himself is
unclear about his own intentions. Like Nietzsche, Foucault
does not engage with those who are inside the practice of legal
punishment and concerned about its details. He is engaged,
it seems, not with such questions as what sentence is appropriate for a given crime or what standard of accountability we
should apply but, rather, with the question of whether we
should punish at all. If Foucault is involved in any justificatory
activity—and he speaks as if he is when he challenges past and
present justifiers—it is that of justifying the whole practice. Is
Foucault, then, a radical critic who tells us why we should not
have the practice of legal punishment?

Foucault often implies that punishment is a practice we
should do without. He says that prisons are "detestable,"[68] and
he suggests that we are in chains:

> "A stupid despot may constrain his slaves with iron
> chains; but a true politician binds them even more
> strongly by the chain of their own ideas; it is at the stable
> point of reason that he secures the end of the chain; this
> link is all the stronger in that we do not know of what it
> is made and we believe it to be our own work."[69]

Moreover, in describing educational institutions as "a relation
of surveillance," Foucault speaks of them as an "insidious
extension" of disciplinary power.[70]

Yet though Foucault is clearly critical of many of our institutions, I do not think he is suggesting that we abolish them,
that we break these odious chains and free ourselves. The use

68. Ibid., p. 232.
69. Ibid., pp. 102–3. This is Foucault's quotation from a work by
Servan.
70. Ibid., p. 176.

of prisons is detestable, but, he adds, "it is the detestable so-
lution which one seems unable to do without."[71] Foucault
gives us no alternatives to the institutions and practices he
claims are coercive.[72] At one point Foucault says that the issue
is not whether we should have prisons but, rather, how we are
to assess the rising use of these mechanisms of normaliza-
tion.[73] It is not the institutions per se that Foucault opposes—
they are but part of "a whole series of carceral mechanisms"
which "all tend, like the prison, to exercise a power of nor-
malization."[74] But where does this leave us with respect to
these practices and institutions? Is Foucault's account in any
sense practical?

In one of his essays in *Power/Knowledge*, Foucault explains
his work as genealogy that gives us a historical knowledge that
we can make use of tactically today.[75] In another essay, a tran-
scription of a discussion he held with Maoists over whether
the institution of a people's court is a good model for the
popular justice the Maoists seek, Foucault opposes the model
of the court; he appeals to his genealogy in arguing that the
idea of a court is opposed to justice. The historic role of penal
systems was "to create mutual antagonisms between the pro-
letarianized common people and the non-proletarianized
common people."[76] The penal system emerged to stamp out
rebellion.[77] Foucault recommends to the Maoists that they give
up on the idea of a court, because courts, and the penal law
they execute, are historically a functioning of power, directed
against those who are politically threatening.[78] Foucault says

71. Ibid., p. 232.
72. For this reason alone we might say he is not engaged in the
activity of justification. One criterion sometimes advanced for giving
a justification is that one must argue for this over that: see Antony
Flew, "The Justification of Punishment," *Philosophy*, vol. 29, no. 111
(October 1954), p. 295.
73. Foucault, *Discipline and Punish*, p. 306.
74. Ibid., pp. 307–8.
75. Foucault, *Power/Knowledge*, p. 83.
76. Ibid., pp. 8–9.
77. Ibid., p. 14.
78. Ibid., p. 15.

that the judicial system and courts must be "the target of our present struggle."[79] The Maoists ask Foucault what form, if not that of the court, popular justice should take. Foucault answers, "[I]t remains to be discovered."[80]

Sometimes Foucault talks as if he does want to cash in practically on his theory of social institutions—he speaks of making tactical use of his genealogy, and of using it in the struggle against existing institutions. But I doubt that he seriously expects or even wants us to abolish our penal system or to abandon the practice of keeping clinical records. Foucault, like Nietzsche, unleashes a radical criticism that smashes our temples today but tomorrow leaves us homeless and still searching. Of course, he may be right that we are not at home in our prisons and asylums.

Both our genealogists, Nietzsche and Foucault, tell us about the origins of our practices. But their efforts are not reducible to a "search for origins."[81] Both have us look at our practices in a new way. Both interpret our practices so that we may understand them in a new light. But their project remains ambiguous: they are unmasking, but to do what? Neither genealogist takes up the questions faced by those inside the practice. Are their projects practical in any sense?

Both at times seem to take up the activity of examining the justification of the practice as a whole, using their radical criticism to deny that the practice is justified. We might ask whether they are successful at this—whether they can persuade us to abolish the practice of legal punishment. But this does not seem a good question, because, as we have seen, neither commits himself to the abolition of the practice. In any case, there is no obvious criterion for success, for deciding whether

79. Ibid., p. 36.
80. Ibid., p. 28.
81. Foucault objects to the effort to reduce Nietzsche's genealogy to the level of a "search for origins" (Michel Foucault, *The Archaeology of Knowledge*, trans. A. M. Sheridan Smith [New York: Pantheon, 1972], p. 13).

they are right about our practices. Nietzsche would tell us that his is but one possible interpretation.[82] I think that to see what is practical in the accounts of these genealogists we must consider the nature of their activity: justifying, or denying the justification of, a practice as a whole. But before we do this, we shall discuss the other radical critics who engage in that activity.

3. Functionalist as Radical Critic: Karl Menninger

A functionalist is someone who explains a practice or institution by giving an account of the function or purpose the practice or institution serves. While functionalists are often justifiers, arguing that an institution that has a useful function is therefore justified by virtue of its function, the functionalist we shall focus on in this section, Karl Menninger, is a radical critic.[83] He suggests that the need legal punishment fulfills is one we would be better off renouncing.[84]

Menninger argues that punishment has its origin in the primitive urge for vengeance and that it functions as an outlet for this urge. Legal punishment is a modern institutional cloak for an instinct Menninger thinks we ought to silence. Though the conclusion he draws differs, Menninger, in linking legal punishment with instinctual drives for vengeance, offers an account of legal punishment similar to several other functionalist accounts of the practice. We will be better able to

82. Nietzsche suggests that at least some of his claims are "conjecture" (*Genealogy*, essay 2, section 6). For an excellent discussion of Nietzsche's perspectivism that explains how for Nietzsche everything is interpretation and also how this perspectivism is not the same as relativism, see Alexander Nehemas, *Nietzsche: Life as Literature* (Cambridge, Mass.: Harvard University Press, 1985).

83. Karl Menninger was one of the most important figures in American psychiatry. The teaching clinic he established in the 1950s trained nearly 15 percent of all psychiatrists schooled in the United States. See Lawrence Friedman, *Menninger* (New York: Alfred A. Knopf, 1990).

84. Karl Menninger, *The Crime of Punishment* (New York: Viking Press, 1966).

focus on what is distinct, and perhaps troubling, about Menninger's account if we first turn to a few of the others.

Some see in revenge the origin of punishment, but an origin whose meaning has been lost and replaced. Hans von Hentig argues that revenge "is the origin of all legal policy and administration of justice."[85] He traces the origin of punishment also to human sacrifice, citing a Brothers Grimm fairy tale, the story of Afzelius, in which two beggar children are buried alive as a sacrifice to end a pestilence.[86] Hentig traces various methods of inflicting punishment to ancient rituals: for example, breaking the criminal on the wheel has its origin in sacrifices to the sun god; punishing the criminal by drowning him is linked to ancient rituals of cleansing.[87] But Hentig argues that the old purposes of punishment are lost. We have only relics.[88] The practice we now have has taken on new purpose.

For Hentig the real function of punishment now is selection and security. Criminal law, in his view, is a "negative selection," a sort of domesticating or breeding of man.[89] Hentig suggests that through capital punishment the criminal type can be weeded out of the gene pool:

> If the untamed, unproductive, the "wild" variety of man gradually disappears, with incessant selection, there will come about a race of men having a socially constructive kind of psychical reactivity.[90]

Hentig, making the assumption that antisocial tendencies can be inherited,[91] also says that sterilization is a means of selection

85. Hans von Hentig, *Punishment: Its Origin, Purpose and Psychology* (1937; reprinted Montclair, N.J.: Patterson Smith, 1973), p. 21.
86. Ibid., p. 39.
87. Ibid., pp. 49–50.
88. Ibid., p. 163.
89. Ibid., pp. 130–31.
90. Ibid., p. 132; cf. pp. 154ff.
91. Ibid., p. 180. For a compelling attack on this assumption and on other tenets of sociobiology, see Stephen Jay Gould, *The Mismeasure of Man* (New York: W. W. Norton, 1981).

and that its power to preserve life and happiness outweighs its harm.[92] Hentig concludes:

> [T]he actual and essential task of penal law is to suppress variants of a worked out social type which are inimical to society.[93]

Hentig's notion that the original purpose of punishment has been lost and that the practice handed down to us has taken on new meaning should remind us of Nietzsche's argument. But not all functionalists accept that the origin of punishment is separate from its function. Emile Durkheim, in his *The Division of Labor in Society*, writes:

> The nature of a practice does not necessarily change because the conscious intentions of those who apply it are modified. It might, in truth, still play the same role as before, but without being perceived. . . . It adapts itself to new conditions of existence without any essential changes. It is so with punishment.[94]

Durkheim, like Hentig and Menninger, thinks that the origin and "essential" character of punishment lie in the seeking of vengeance.[95] But for Durkheim, the original purpose of punishment has not been lost. Durkheim opposes those such as Hentig who claim that punishment has changed its character and that "it is no longer to avenge itself that society punishes,

92. Ibid., pp. 146–47.
93. Ibid., p. 158.
94. Emile Durkheim, *The Division of Labor in Society*, trans. George Simpson (1893; reprinted Glencoe, Ill.: Free Press, 1933), p. 87.
95. The idea that there is an "essential" character to punishment should trouble us. Much of my argument is premised on the fact that there are no essential criteria that make a thing punishment; punishment is a concept with "blurred edges." However, in thinking about the practical problems arising in legal punishment I employ an interpretation of the practice that claims to capture best what punishment essentially is. But as a nonfoundationalist and a critic of essentialism, I must qualify this claim by acknowledging that it is but an interpretation. See my discussion in chapter 5.

it is to defend itself."[96] Durkheim's response is subtle: those who claim punishment has changed think of vengeance as useless cruelty and see in our own punishment a useful practice. But

> it is an error to believe that vengeance is but useless cruelty. It is very possible that, in itself, it consists of a mechanical and aimless reaction, in an emotional and irrational movement, in an unintelligent need to destroy; but, in fact, what it tends to destroy was a menace to us. It consists, then, in a veritable act of defense, although an instinctive and unreflective one. . . . Today, since we better understand the end to be attained, we better know how to utilize the means at our disposal; we protect ourselves with better means and, accordingly, more efficiently. But, in the beginning, this result was obtained in a rather imperfect manner.[97]

The essential elements of punishment are the same as of old.[98] Punishment is an act of vengeance, but we now know that in this act of vengeance society protects itself: "What we avenge, what the criminal expiates, is the outrage to morality."[99] Where Nietzsche and Hentig sever the ties of genealogy and functionalism, of origin and purpose, then, Durkheim combines the two in justifying the practice of legal punishment.

Another thinker who connects genealogy with functionalism for, it seems to me, the sake of justifying the practice of legal punishment is René Girard. Girard recounts the story of Cain and Abel to illustrate his own story about why we punish. Abel regularly sacrifices the firstborn of his herds. His brother Cain "does not have the violence-outlet of animal sacrifice at his disposal."[100] Lacking this outlet, Cain channels his violence

96. Durkheim, *The Division of Labor in Society*, pp. 86–87.
97. Ibid., p. 87.
98. Ibid., p. 88; cf. p. 90.
99. Ibid., p. 89. It is important to note that Durkheim does not mean that the origin of punishment is the private vendetta: "It is far from true that private vengeance is the prototype of punishment; it is, on the contrary, only an imperfect punishment" (p. 94).
100. René Girard, *Violence and the Sacred*, trans. Patrick Gregory (1972; Baltimore: Johns Hopkins University Press, 1977), p. 4.

into the murder of his brother. Girard's point is that we punish as an outlet for our instinctual, violent urges. In many primitive societies lacking legal punishment, sacrifice provides this outlet. The sacrificial victim is on the margin.[101] Her death puts an end to the acts of vengeance that disrupt society. The death of the victim does not entail an act of vengeance precisely because the victim—a scapegoat—is not integrated, has no social links, no one to avenge her sacrifice.[102] Sacrifice saves society, which would otherwise self-destruct, by curbing the otherwise endless chain of acts of vengeance.

Girard argues that in our society the judicial system limits vengeance to a single act, which becomes the final word; we have "public vengeance."[103] "Our penal system operates according to principles of justice that are in no real conflict with the concept of revenge." It is a system of "violent retribution."[104] Legal punishment, in this view, differs from revenge because it puts an end to vengeance, as did sacrifice in primitive society.[105] Modern legal punishment is a functional equivalent to primitive sacrifices and religion.[106] The legal system conceals its resemblance to acts of vengeance by forging its retribution into "a principle of abstract justice that all men are obliged to uphold and respect."[107] What is concealed is that "the penal system owes its origins to generative violence" and not to some "rational agreement on a sort of social contract."[108]

Girard says that his purpose is "to expose to the light of reason the role played by violence in human society."[109] In this respect he resembles the genealogists we have already considered. But although Girard is in a way unmasking, I do not think he is giving us a radical criticism, as the genealogists

101. Ibid., p. 12.
102. Ibid., p. 13.
103. Ibid., p. 15.
104. Ibid., p. 16.
105. Ibid., p. 17.
106. Ibid., p. 18.
107. Ibid., pp. 21–22.
108. Ibid., p. 298.
109. Ibid., p. 318.

appear to do, and as we shall see that Menninger does. Rather, Girard tends, like Durkheim, to show us what is positive in our practices, as Hentig also thinks himself to be doing. Girard notes that sacrifice is a real purification, because it curbs real violence. Sacrifice and its functional equivalent, legal punishment, serve a terribly important function, a function essential for the preservation of society: "The slightest outbreak of violence can bring about a catastrophic escalation."[110] It is because of its destructive capacity that violence is sacred in many primitive societies, just like other things that spread—fire, plague, storms.[111]

Girard, like Durkheim, focuses our attention on what is positive in a practice we might otherwise think cruel. He is not engaged in justifying actions within the practice; if he is engaged in any justificatory activity, it is the justification of the practice as a whole, the question all the thinkers we are considering in this chapter seem to take up. Like the radical critics, Girard tries to get us to see our practice in a new way; he gives an interpretation. His interpretation differs from that of another justifier of punishment, Hentig, and it differs from that of the genealogists we considered. Now we shall see how it differs from that of Karl Menninger.[112]

Menninger, like the other functionalists, links punishment and revenge, but he draws conclusions different from theirs. Menninger is critical—we sense this already from the title of his book: *The Crime of Punishment*.

Menninger says that legal punishment is motivated by zeal for inflicting pain.[113] To him the justifications we give for the practice only mask our desire to punish: "We disown violence but we really love it."[114] Though we may say we punish to

110. Ibid., p. 30.
111. Ibid., p. 31.
112. It should be troubling not only that there are such conflicting views about punishment's origin and function, but that even those who *do* agree arrive at such different conclusions about the practice. I shall consider this point in section 5, below.
113. Menninger, *The Crime of Punishment*, p. 113.
114. Ibid., p. 162.

deter or incapacitate, in punishing we actually seek revenge. Menninger follows Freud in seeing violence as innate. It is something to which we are attracted and which we romanticize.[115] We have an instinct for destructiveness; we save our own lives "by destroying something external."[116] Those who commit crimes of violence are not alone: Menninger says we all have this instinct for destructiveness. Most of us find ways to sublimate it; for example, some of us play chess:

> The picture of two individuals sitting, peacefully regarding a piece-studded board, is misleading. Silently their men are plotting and attempting to execute murderous campaigns of patricide, matricide, fratricide, regicide, and mayhem.[117]

Menninger's point about violence being innate is twofold: he says we are all subject to the temptations of crime, and therefore our worst crime is "damning some of our fellow citizens with the label of criminal";[118] and he also contends that our urge to punish reflects the same instincts that motivate the criminal.

Instead of drawing what seems to be Girard's conclusion— that legal punishment is justified because it puts an end to the cycle of revenge—Menninger sees punishment as *part* of the "endless cycle of evil for evil" and counsels us to end this cycle by no longer punishing. We should "shed our thirst for vengeance, grow ashamed of our cry for retaliation, and repudiate vengeance as a human motive."[119] Menninger's exemplar is the father who, though his daughter was killed, yet was strong enough to silence his natural instinct and, in a letter to the editor, write: "Let no feelings of cave-man vengeance

115. Ibid., pp. 190, 157–62.
116. Ibid., p. 163.
117. Ibid., p. 169. Menninger cites an article by Ernest Jones on the psychoanalysis of chess, in *International Journal of Psychoanalysis*, vol. 12 (1931), pp. 1–23.
118. Menninger, *The Crime of Punishment*, p. 9.
119. Ibid., p. 280.

influence us. Let us rather help him who did so human a thing."[120]

When Menninger says we should not punish, he sounds like a radical critic calling for the abolition of the practice. He challenges the ideal underlying the criminal justice system, calling this justice "hypocritical" or "beside the point."[121] But sometimes Menninger implies that he does not want to abolish the practice. He argues that it is unfair to treat all as equal, as justice dictates:

> Freud showed that men are extremely unequal in respect to endowment, discretion, equilibrium, self-control, aspiration and intelligence . . . differences depending not only on inherited genes and brain-cell configurations but also on childhood conditioning.[122]

After Freud, nothing could be more unfair than treating all as equal.[123] The law is premised on the "reasonable man." Menninger asks, "[W]hat of the irrational?"[124] And so he proposes specific reforms of our practice: for example, individualized sentencing[125] and an increase in the number of parole and probation officers.[126] Menninger's ideal is treatment, not punishment; more mental hospitals, fewer prisons.[127]

Menninger's position is unclear. Sometimes he stands outside the practice, attacking the very idea of legal punishment, as when he calls criminal justice a "scapegoat system" and a "morality play";[128] but sometimes he stands inside the practice, calling for reforms that would change the way we inflict punishment. This confusion stems in part from a conceptual

120. Ibid., p. 199.
121. Ibid., pp. 153–54.
122. Ibid., p. 92.
123. Ibid.
124. Ibid., p. 94.
125. Ibid., pp. 63, 70.
126. Ibid., p. 87.
127. Ibid., p. 93.
128. Ibid., pp. 153–54.

confusion in Menninger's views about punishment. When Menninger attacks punishment, he means by "punishment" the vengeful infliction of pain or "long-continued torture."[129] In his view punishment is opposed to treatment; punishment is something hateful; and so when Menninger counsels "love against hate," he, by his own stipulation, excludes punishment.[130] Menninger forgets that it is possible to punish those we love—parents do this all the time. Menninger slaps ordinary language in the face when he insists that punishment means "pain inflicted over years for the sake of inflicting pain."[131]

By his own definition, Menninger would not call "punishment" his own proposal for dealing with criminals: commitment to a mental hospital for treatment. Menninger is not the only one sharply to separate "punishment" and "treatment."[132] We ought to find the distinction troublesome. ("Of course someone committed to a mental hospital is being punished." "But we're helping him, not punishing him." "But the state has coerced him, as it coerces convicts.") We can select a method of inflicting punishment that is not painful but which we still call punishment by virtue of its being part of the practice of punishment as a whole. Later, when we take an internal approach to punishment—something I think Menninger at least sometimes implicitly does—we will say that perhaps Menninger is not challenging from the outside the whole practice of legal punishment (though unfortunately his rhetoric suggests this) but that he is on the inside, challenging certain subpractices, namely, how we sentence, and how we inflict punishment. Had he explicitly taken this approach, Menninger

129. Ibid., pp. 218, 202.
130. Ibid., ch. 10.
131. Ibid., p. 202.
132. Cf. Sutherland and Cressey: "The confinement of a psychotic person may involve suffering for him, but it is not punishment. Many of the modern methods of dealing with criminals, especially juvenile court procedures, are not punitive" (Edwin Sutherland and Donald Cressey, *Criminology*, 8th ed. [Philadelphia: J. B. Lippincott, 1970], p. 298).

could have denounced certain methods of inflicting punishment while affirming the practice of legal punishment on the whole.

If we emphasize the passages in which Menninger says the real reason we punish is to express our instinct for vengeance and suggests that all other justifications for punishment are ideological smokescreens hiding this instinctual motive, then Menninger does appear to be a radical critic. He explains our practice as an outlet for primitive emotions we should now all have outgrown. If we take him as a radical critic—though this might be to take too seriously what is either his rhetoric, or his confusion over a word—we are left asking how persuasive his account is. It seems troublesome that this functionalist comes to such a very different conclusion from that of his fellow functionalists, who affirm the practice. How are we to decide which account is best? How can there be so many "explanations" of the same practice? As before, I defer answering until we have given all of our radical critics a hearing.

4. Marxist as Radical Critic

Karl Marx wrote little directly on the subject of crime and punishment. But from his theoretical project was spun an entire literature of radical criminology, which interprets punishment with the help of the vision Marx's theory lends. This literature is essentially critical of punishment. Marxists deny not only the justness of, but also the conventional justifications given for, legal punishment.[133] The Marxists we shall consider are radical critics—they stand outside of the practice.

133. Marx scholars tend to distinguish Marxists from Marxians, the latter being more or less faithful to Marx's texts, the former diverging in significant ways, to the point even of vulgarizing Marx. Because I am not concerned, here, with how faithful to Marx's texts these radical critics are, I shall be content calling them "Marxists." On the distinction, see Paul Thomas, "Marx's Reception: Then and Now," in Terrell Carver, ed., *Cambridge Companion to Philosophy: Karl Marx* (Cambridge: Cambridge University Press, forthcoming).

In an article written for the *New York Daily Tribune* on capital punishment, Marx makes clear enough his understanding of the practice of legal punishment as a whole:

> Plainly speaking, and dispensing with all paraphrases, punishment is nothing but a means of society to defend itself against the infraction of its vital conditions, whatever may be their character. Now, what a state of society is that which knows of no better instrument for its own defense than the hangman, and which proclaims through the "leading journal of the world" [*The Times*] its own brutality as eternal law?[134]

In this passage Marx is making a claim and a judgment. The judgment is that punishment is brutal. The claim Marx makes is the core claim of radical criminologists: that punishment is an instrument used by society to defend itself so that it may maintain itself—punishment is useful in preserving society. What Marx barely hints at here, but which is central to the Marxist argument, is that it is precisely because of its use that punishment is unjust.

The Marxist (to generalize) understands capitalist society to be divided between two classes, the property-owning bourgeoisie and the propertyless proletariat. The state, with its legal and political apparatus, claims to represent the interests of all members of society, but in fact it allows the property-owning class to perpetuate its unjust domination over the propertyless. A typical version of the Marxist argument goes like this:

> The legal system is an apparatus that is created to secure the interests of the dominant class. Contrary to conventional belief, law is a tool of the ruling class. The legal system provides the mechanism for the forceful and violent control of the rest of the population. In the course of the battle, the agents of the law serve as the military

134. Karl Marx, "Capital Punishment," in *New York Daily Tribune*, February 18, 1853, in Karl Marx and Friedrich Engels, *Gesamtausgabe* (MEGA) (Berlin: Dietz, 1984), vol. 12, pp. 25–26.

force for the protection of domestic order. Hence, the state and its accompanying legal system reflect and serve the needs of the ruling class. The primary interest of the ruling class is to preserve the existing capitalist order. . . . This is accomplished ultimately by means of the legal system.[135]

Radical criminologists see criminal law and law enforcement as useful, but only to the powerful interests and dominant classes of society.[136] They see in crime a political act:

> When we say that all inmates are political prisoners, we are not asserting that all criminal acts are deliberate, self-conscious acts of rebellion against an unjust authority. In fact, the overwhelming majority of inmates we saw are doing time for narrow, selfish acts such as stealing, breaking and entering, and fighting. Nevertheless, their incarceration is political since it is the end-product of decisions to treat some social harms as deserving of penal sanctions and others as not—with little regard to the actual extent of social damage.[137]

This passage indicates a more refined Marxism that avoids explaining *every* aspect of the criminal justice system by class analysis. Not all Marxist criminologists hold that *all* law serves the interests only of powerful elites, or that the state is nothing

135. Richard Quinney, "Crime Control in Capitalist Society," in Ian Taylor, Paul Walton, and Jock Young, eds., *Critical Criminology* (London: Routledge and Kegan Paul, 1975), pp. 192–93, 195.

136. Cf. Barry Krisberg, *Power and Privilege: Toward a New Criminology* (Englewood Cliffs, N.J.: Prentice-Hall, 1975); Richard Quinney, *The Social Reality of Crime* (Boston: Little, Brown, 1970); William Chambliss and Robert Seidman, *Law, Order, and Power* (Reading, Mass.: Addison-Wesley, 1971). For a bibliography see David F. Greenberg, ed., *Crime and Capitalism: Readings in Marxist Criminology* (Palo Alto: Mayfield Publishing, 1981).

137. Joan Smith and William Fried, *The Uses of the American Prison: Political Theory and Penal Practice* (Lexington: Lexington Books, 1974), cited in Greenberg, ed., *Crime and Capitalism*, pp. 8–9. In chapter 4 I shall consider in detail the concept of political crime.

but an instrument of a cohesive ruling class. Some explicitly deny such a view, arguing that it would be a mistake to think

> that all laws represent the interests of persons in power at the expense of persons less influential. In many cases there is no conflict whatsoever between those in power and those not. For most crimes against the person, such as murder, assault, and rape, there is consensus through-out society as to the desirability of imposing legal sanctions for persons who commit these acts.[138]

More refined Marxists interpret the practice of legal punishment in a capitalist society as *on the whole* a tool of oppression used by one class against another.

All Marxists see the criminal laws punishment enforces as serving to protect the system of private property essential to capitalism:

> Crime is a direct or indirect assault on the interests of private property in a bourgeois society, thus on the core of capitalist exploitation and class domination of the bourgeoisie.[139]

> Basically, that is to say from the purely sociological standpoint, the bourgeoisie maintains its class rule and suppresses the exploited classes by means of its system of criminal law.[140]

Some Marxists emphasize that the penal system is not merely a bourgeois phenomenon, but reflects class interests whatever they may be. Pashukanis, for example, writes:

138. William Chambliss, *Crime and Legal Process* (New York: McGraw-Hill, 1969), p. 10, cited in Greenberg, ed., *Crime and Capitalism*, p. 29, note 27.

139. Andrej A. Piontkowski, *Hegels Lehre über Staat und Recht und seine Strafrechtstheorie*, trans. from the Russian by Anna Neuland (Berlin: VEB Deutscher Zentralverlag, 1960), pp. 157–58.

140. Evgeny B. Pashukanis, *Law and Marxism*, trans. Barbara Einhorn (1929; reprinted London: Ink Links, 1978), p. 173.

Every historically given system of penal policy bears the imprint of the class interests of that class which instigated it. The feudal lord had intractable peasants and towns-people who opposed his power executed. The confederate cities hung the robber knights and destroyed their strongholds. In the Middle Ages, every person who tried to follow a trade without being a member of the guild was thought to be a law-breaker.[141]

The particular features of the penal system in capitalist society reflect that society's class structure. Pashukanis argues that the emphasis in our penal system on an individual's intentions and our use of prison sentences to make punishment commensurable with the crime are both bourgeois phenomena. "Primitive" penal laws, argues Pashukanis, don't recognize the requirement of *mens rea* (intent) for criminal liability:

If an animal from a herd of sheep, cattle or horses—so it says in a description of the customs of the [present-day] Ossetians—knocks a stone down from the mountain, and this stone injures or kills someone passing by, then the relatives of the injured or dead person pursue the owner of the animal with their blood vengeance—just as though it were a premeditated act of murder.[142]

The notion of individual guilt "corresponds to the radical in-dividualism of bourgeois society."[143] Pashukanis argues also that the idea of punishment as an "equivalence" for the crime is a product of a thought-structure distinctly bourgeois:

Deprivation of freedom, for a period stipulated in the court sentence, is the specific form in which modern, that is to say bourgeois-capitalist, criminal law embodies the principle of equivalent recompense. This form is un-consciously yet deeply linked with the conception of man in the abstract, and abstract human labour measurable in time. It is no coincidence that this form of punishment

141. Ibid., p. 174.
142. Ibid., p. 178, note 19.
143. Ibid., p. 178.

became established precisely in the 19th century, and was considered natural. . . . Prisons and dungeons did exist in ancient times and in the Middle Ages too. . . . But people were usually held there until their death, or until they bought themselves free. For it to be possible for the idea to emerge that one could make recompense for an offense with a piece of abstract freedom determined in advance, it was necessary for all concrete forms of social wealth to be reduced to the most abstract and simple form, to human labour measured in time.[144]

Pashukanis, in pointing to how particular aspects of modern penal practice reflect the modern relations of the means of production, expands on a point Marx and Engels had made in arguing that crime in a capitalist society is itself a creation of bourgeois society. In his *Tribune* article Marx writes,

It is not so much the particular political institutions of a country as the fundamental conditions of modern bourgeois society in general, which produce an average amount of crime in a given national fraction of society.

Engels draws the conclusion that without bourgeois society there would be no crime, hence no need for punishment:

Crimes against property cease of their own accord where everyone receives what he needs to satisfy his natural and his spiritual urges, where social gradations and distinctions cease to exist. Justice concerned with criminal cases ceases of itself . . . conflicts can then be only rare exceptions, whereas they are now the natural result of general hostility.[145]

Although some Marxists see themselves as only *explaining* the emergence and significance of punishment in a capitalist

144. Ibid., pp. 180–81.
145. Engels, "Speech in Elberfeld," February 8, 1845, in Marx and Engels, *Collected Works*, 44 vols. (London: Lawrence and Wishart, 1975), vol. 4, pp. 248–49. Cf. Pashukanis, *Law and Marxism*, p. 175: "[I]t is very doubtful whether [with the complete disappearance of classes] there will be any necessity at all for a penal system."

society, most radical criminologists *judge* the practice of legal punishment to be unjust. The law that is enforced is unjust, for it serves to protect only the ruling class, and the punishment unleashed to enforce laws upholding unjust property relations is unjust as well:

> There is something perverse in applying [retributive] principles that presuppose a sense of community in a society which is structured to destroy genuine community. . . . Criminals typically are not members of a shared community of values with their jailers, they suffer from what Marx calls alienation.[146]

The Marxist is a skeptic. And his skepticism is of the whole practice. Marxists, in general, are aiming their criticism not at the brutality of punishment per se, as Marx himself does in his article on capital punishment, but, rather, at the whole practice of legal punishment. Although some with a Marxist bent challenge the selective enforcement by police of criminal laws that result in mainly the poor going to jail, or challenge particular vagrancy laws as blatant examples of law serving the interests of property owners,[147] on the whole the Marxist is attacking not particular laws but the whole practice of legal punishment under capitalism, and beyond this, the whole structure of capitalist society. For Pashukanis, the overthrow of the "legal form"—the whole set of assumptions about legal personality, individual guilt, and commensurability that underlie modern penal practice—depends on "transcending the framework of bourgeois society, but also on a radical eman-

146. Jeffrie Murphy, "Marxism and Retribution," *Philosophy and Public Affairs*, vol. 2, no. 3 (Spring 1973), pp. 239–40.
147. For example, the *New York Times*, November 4, 1988, reported that in response to the problem of homelessness, the police force of the city of Miami has proposed a new law making it a misdemeanor punishable by ten days in jail or a hundred-dollar fine or both to sleep, cook, bathe, or urinate on a public right of way, which includes sidewalks and parks. This proposal emerged partly because downtown shopowners say they are tired of having potential customers scared away by street people.

cipation from all its remnants."[148] Radical criminology is indeed radical: it attacks the practice at its roots. The Marxist thinks our practices are bad through and through, and criticizes them from the outside. In contrast, the immanent critic believes that our practices are, on the whole, just, and stands inside a practice to criticize it by principles already there.

Sometimes it seems there is no ground shared between the Marxist critic and the practitioner of legal punishment. Consider the argument made by a group of British Marxist criminologists about mugging. In their view, mugging is a crime constructed by the police, courts, and media as a response to a crisis of legitimacy:

> We believe, then, that the nature of the reaction to "mugging" can only be understood in terms of the way society—more especially the ruling-class alliances, the state apparatuses and the media—responded to a deepening economic, political and social crisis.[149]

In this view, the crisis of mugging, created in the late 1960s and early 1970s, was a cloak to mask the political nature of the real problem, that of structural and racial inequality.[150] Crime is political revenge by "an excluded black group in a dominant white world."[151] The suggestion that mugging is somehow constructed—not really a wrong, but a political expression of injustice—will be hard for anyone to accept who is at home in the practices of our capitalist society. To such people, the Marxist critic speaks a foreign language. Similarly, radical criminologists tend to dismiss the language spoken by justifiers inside the practice. Like Foucault, some Marxists do not take reformers of the Enlightenment at their word. They see reform as due, not to humanitarian ideals of enlightened

148. Pashukanis, *Law and Marxism*, p. 64.
149. Stuart Hall, Chas Critcher, Tony Jefferson, John Clarke, and Brian Roberts, *Policing the Crisis: Mugging, the State, and Law and Order* (London: Macmillan Press, 1978), p. 306; cf. pp. viii, 177, 216–17. Cf. my discussion in chapter 1, section 1.
150. Ibid., pp. 118–19.
151. Ibid., p. 359.

individuals, but to pressure from capitalists who seek to protect their property.[152] They are skeptical of the motives of reformers, and this skepticism reflects a skepticism of the whole practice:

> Liberal reformism in criminology supports the extension of Welfare State capitalism and gradualist programmes of amelioration, whilst rejecting radical and violent forms of social and political change. . . . This kind of reformism has helped to create probation and parole, the juvenile court system, reformations and half-way houses, the indeterminate sentence, adjustment and diagnostic centres, public defenders, youth service bureaus and many other "reforms" which have served to strengthen the power of the State over the poor, third-world communities, and youth.[153]

Another well-known example of a Marxist account imputes "underlying motives" to past justifiers, who are therefore not taken at their word. Otto Kirchheimer and Georg Rusche argue that penal methods are determined by basic social relations and that punishment is not a logical consequence of crime but a social phenomenon in its own right, a phenomenon that varies with the productive relations of a society.[154] They explain the reform era by pointing to the need of the bourgeoisie for legal guarantees of their own security against the authorities.[155] The distinctive feature of the theory of Kirchheimer and Rusche is its account of why society inflicts punishment the way that it does. They argue that prior to the growth of prisons, punishment was corporal and cruel because there was no labor shortage and the penal system could be

152. See Michael Rustigan, "A Reinterpretation of Criminal Law Reform in 19th Century England," in Greenberg, ed., *Crime and Capitalism*, pp. 255–78.
153. Tony Platt, "Prospects for a Radical Criminology in the USA," in Taylor, Walton, and Young, eds., *Critical Criminology*, pp. 95–112.
154. Otto Kirchheimer and Georg Rusche, *Punishment and Social Structure* (New York: Russell and Russell, 1939), p. 5.
155. Ibid., pp. 72–74.

used to prevent too great an increase in population.[156] By the end of the sixteenth century demand for labor had increased and, as a result, the ruling class turned to prison labor.[157] With the industrial revolution and the consequent rise in population and spread of factories, prison labor was no longer competitive, and so imprisonment was no longer justified as a source of labor; and, because crime was rising as a consequence of industrialization, punishment became justified as a means of deterrence—punishment now had to hurt.[158] Implicit in this argument is the notion of "objective justifications" that explain the evolution of the practice apart from the actual justifications given by past justifiers.

What can the practitioner say to such arguments? How would they pass muster at a town meeting about whether to build a new jail? To be sure, there are important differences among the radical criminologists, and I have no doubt distorted or inadequately characterized the subtle views of some by grouping them together with others as "Marxists." But our purpose here is not to catch these subtleties. Rather, it is to see the character of their critical activity, to see whether they give us a theory that is in any sense practical.

The Marxist is not engaged in justifying actions within the practice of legal punishment. He does not help us in the numerous practical decisions we must make every day.

> How can Marx help us with our real practical problem? The answer, I think, is that he cannot and obviously does not desire to do so. For Marx would say that we have not focused on what is truly the real problem. And this is changing the basic social relations.[159]

One radical criminologist explains his conception of his activity:

156. Ibid., p. 20.
157. Ibid., pp. 25, 29.
158. Ibid., pp. 95–113.
159. Murphy, "Marxism and Retribution," p. 242.

Our comprehension of the present, as well as the past, is mystified by a consciousness that only serves to maintain the existing order. Only with a new consciousness— a critical philosophy—can we begin to realize the world of which we are capable . . . any possibility for a different life will come about only through new ideas that are formed in the course of altering the way we think and the way we live. What is involved here is no less than a whole new way of life. What is necessary is a new beginning—intellectually, spiritually and politically.[160]

The Marxist is not at home in our practice of legal punishment. He calls us to a "new way of life," with "a new beginning." The Marxist is a radical critic. Like the other radical critics, the Marxist smashes our temples. Like some of the others, he does this so that we may build a new home.

We have examined several radical critics who are engaged in the activity of justifying the whole practice of legal punishment and who deny that the practice is justified. Now we must see how we can judge whether they are right.

5. The Activity of Justifying a Whole Practice

The radical critics we have examined take up the question, "Why do we have the practice of legal punishment?" They seem to be explaining: the genealogist explains how our practice emerged; the functionalist explains the purpose or function our practice now serves. Both are telling us *why* we have the practice.

Yet I've called them radical *critics*. They seem not merely to explain *why* we punish, as if their purpose were simply to increase our store of knowledge, but to argue for or against legal punishment as a practice. Menninger and at least some Marxists explicitly advocate abolishing legal punishment, and both Nietzsche and Foucault establish themselves as critics of the practice. But how do we get from explanation to justifi-

160. Quinney, "Crime Control in Capitalist Society," p. 181.

cation? If we know, from either the genealogist's or the functionalist's account, why we have the practice, do we therefore know that we should (not) continue to have it? do we then have its justification?

Explanations, or accounts of the origin or cause of a practice, can be important in shaping our understanding of a practice and its justification. For example, someone who observes a religious taboo against eating pork, perhaps because she believes that violating the taboo will result in her suffering divine retribution, perhaps simply because it is her family's or community's tradition not to eat pork, might rethink her reasons for avoiding pork if persuaded by an anthropologist that in fact the taboo was created not by her god but by some leader long ago who realized that in the arid terrain where her religious ancestors once dwelled, pigs are difficult to raise (pigs don't sweat); and because pork is so succulent, absent a proscription against eating it, the people would be tempted to raise pigs and would thus waste scarce economic resources.[161] On the other hand, our pork abstainer might *not* be convinced by this explanation of the origin of the taboo. She has her reasons for complying with it, and they might satisfy her. She might fail to see why the anthropologist's explanation should compel her to give up her own reasons for not eating pork.

In presenting themselves as explainers with special insight into an essence beneath the appearances of our practice, and in refusing to take at face value the reasons given by those inside the practice of legal punishment, the radical critics distance themselves from the subjects of their explanations, and this distance becomes disenabling, posing a significant obstacle that limits the practical effect the radical critic can have. Two problems in particular are associated with this critical distance, problems that amount to barriers for those who want

161. Marvin Harris gives such an ecological account of the cause of the taboo, though he makes no reference to a leader ever consciously creating a myth to get the people to comply with the taboo (*Cows, Pigs, Wars, and Witches* [New York: Random House, 1974], "Pig Lovers and Pig Haters").

to leap from explanation to justification (or criticism): the radical critics fail (1) to consider practical alternatives to punishment, and (2) to engage in dialogue with those inside the practice.

Justifiers typically argue for this over that: we should, rather than not, criminalize marijuana use; this woman, not that, should be indicted; he should be executed, not imprisoned for life. Most of our radical critics generate in us a skepticism about our practices but leave us without any alternatives, and thus in a rather confusing and troubling position. I have suggested that Nietzsche and Foucault put us in this position. When the Maoists Foucault counsels ask, "If not penal institutions, then what?" Foucault answers, "It remains to be discovered."

Menninger does offer us an alternative: treatment, not punishment. But, as I have suggested, insofar as Menninger counsels us to use more mental hospitals and fewer prisons he assumes a position inside the practice, justifying how we should sentence and inflict punishment. At this point in his argument he is not an external skeptic challenging our whole temple, but an internal critic trying to fix it. To argue with him about the substance of his criticism would require us to assume a position within the practice (which we shall do when we take an internal approach) and debate with him about alternative methods of inflicting punishment.

Some Marxists who challenge the whole practice of legal punishment also offer us an alternative: a new society. Lenin, in *State and Revolution*, describes a society in which the state—which he defines as the police and the standing army—disappears, and, with it, crime and punishment. But is this alternative practical? Surely there will be some antisocial activity even in a society without private property.[162] How does

162. Marxists have been accused of being utopian in asserting that crime and repression will disappear in socialist society. Some accuse them of neglecting the persistence of crime and punishment in existing socialist countries: See Greenberg, ed., *Crime and Capitalism*, pp. 22–25; and Gwynn Nettler, *Explaining Crime* (2d ed. New York: McGraw-Hill, 1978).

Lenin think society will respond without its mechanisms of criminal justice in place?

> We are not utopians, and do not in the least deny the possibility and inevitability of excesses by *individual persons*, or the need to suppress *such* excesses. But, in the first place, no special machine, no special apparatus of suppression is needed for this; it will be done by the armed people itself, as simply and as readily as any crowd of civilized people, even in modern society, interferes to put a stop to a scuffle or to prevent a woman from being assaulted.[163]

This will hardly be persuasive to those of us familiar with stories of women being raped on subways in New York City in the middle of rush hour while the crowd looks away. Of course, the Marxist or Leninist would respond that the fear or apathy of people riding New York City subways is a product of the pathological institutions and practices inherent in our capitalist society. Whether we think their arguments are practical will turn on whether we think this fear or apathy results from capitalism, and, more than this, on whether we think that concern for and trust of others could be reinfused by a social and economic transformation away from capitalism.

Lenin offers another suggestion for how society will deal with deviant behavior:

> For when *all* have learned to administer and actually do independently administer social production, independently keep accounts and exercise control over the parasites, the sons of privilege, the swindlers and suchlike "guardians of capitalist traditions," the escape from this popular accounting and control will inevitably become so incredibly difficult, such a rare exception, and will probably be accompanied by such swift and severe punishment (for the armed workers are practical people and not sentimental intellectuals, and they will scarcely allow anyone to trifle with them), that the *necessity* of observing

163. V. I. Lenin, *The State and Revolution* (Peking: Foreign Language Press, 1976), p. 110, Lenin's emphasis.

the simple, fundamental rules of all human community life will very soon become a *habit*.[164]

It seems that punishment will remain, but absent the due-process guarantees of our practice, it hardly seems more appealing than our present system. Nor does Lenin explain why even with this new "habit" there won't be deviants, given that we have habits too, yet lots of people break them from time to time.

Crime happens here and now. Its victims, actual and potential, experience its immediacy and demand an appropriate response, here and now. By moving beyond (or beneath) the here and now for critical perspective, most of the radical critics we have considered fail to take seriously the immediacy and urgency of the problems occupying those of us inside the practice of legal punishment. The radical critic suggests to us that we should not punish at all; but if not punishment, then what? What is to be done with those who commit crimes *now*, in *this* (and not some future, transformed) society?

A second feature typical of justifications is the engagement in dialogue with those who dispute the justifier. One reason this is absent from our radical critics' accounts is, simply enough, that unlike most practitioners when engaged in justification, our radical critics write books; they don't have immediately to answer objections or reformulate their arguments. Beyond this, radical critics stand outside the practice and aren't forced to "speak the language" of practitioners. The radical critic isn't committed to the practice she criticizes. She doesn't share many of the assumptions implicit in the practice. Indeed, it may be that no common ground is shared between her and the practitioner. Consider a city council meeting convened to discuss whether a new vagrancy law should be passed, such as the one advocated by shop owners in Miami that would punish street people who sleep, cook, bathe, or urinate on a public right of way.[165] A Marxist speaking at the meeting might say something like:

164. Ibid., p. 124.
165. Cf. note 147 above.

To preserve your temples of commerce you deny the most fundamental of human needs. Yet again your insatiable craving for profits prevents you from seeing that it is precisely for the fulfillment of human needs that we must replace with a new the old caste of priests running your temples of exploitation. This law is but another example of how the ruling class of capitalists uses the machinery of state punishment, which it has acquired through its expropriation of surplus value, to oppress the marginalized proletariat.

How would this go over with the concerned citizenry? I suspect they would not *understand* our Marxist, though probably they would feel threatened by her words. By saying the radical critic does not speak the language of the practitioner I mean, not only that she uses for rhetorical ends a terminology that sounds foreign, but that she looks at everyday things—the state, the store owner, the vagrant, the shop, the practice of legal punishment—in a way unfamiliar to those at home in capitalist society and its practices. Her language and standpoint make it difficult for those on the inside to engage in dialogue with her.

Many of our radical critics insist that their explanations are true in some absolute sense and cast doubt on, if not the intentions, then the capacity for self-understanding of past justifiers. We saw this to be the case with Foucault, Menninger, and Marxists, all of whom suggest that justifications are "objective" and none of whom take Enlightenment penal reformers at their word. Since in practice justification involves the defense of an action against the charges made by someone else (or by ourselves, if we are divided), it seems essential that there be at least the possibility for dialogue, but our radical critics—perhaps only for rhetorical purposes, perhaps because their vision is so radical that for lack of common ground we can't engage in the give and take of dialogue with them—sometimes close off this possibility.

Still, what if our radical critics are *right* that our practices are bad root and branch? Perhaps they are right that those inside the practice are either deceivers or deceived and that the truth about our practices is learned, not from the understanding practitioners have, but only by digging beneath the surface. But can we speak of truth here? Each of the radical critics we considered answers the question "Why do we have the practice of legal punishment?" We have seen how much room there is for various interpretations of this question. What criteria have we for choosing from among them that which is true?

Many of our radical critics link punishment with revenge, but they understand revenge in different ways. For Nietzsche, revenge is for the sickly and weak, something to be despised. For Durkheim, revenge is different from the private vendetta; it is a reaction of the social consciousness, and through the act of vengeance we uphold the social morality. For Menninger, revenge is what Durkheim explicitly says it is not: useless cruelty. Although his reasoning is different, Menninger comes to the same conclusion as Nietzsche: revenge is something we should be strong enough to renounce. (Unlike Menninger, Nietzsche thinks the revenge of retributive punishment is not rooted in our instinctual or natural will.) For Girard, revenge is destructive though instinctual cruelty, but is *stopped* by punishment. How are we to decide which view is right?

To answer this question, I think we must reflect upon the nature of the activity of justifying a whole practice. In our previous discussion we noted that in justifying actions that belong to a practice, one can use criteria that derive from the practice: for example, its rules, rules of thumb, principles, strategies, and an interpretation of the point of the practice. But it is unclear from where standards come in justifying practices.[166] When we justify a practice as a whole, we ask ourselves whether we are at home in it. Our answer will depend partly on our understanding, or interpretation, of the practice. An interpretation may rest on an elaborate vision of society, as do Foucault's and that of the Marxists, or on a more narrow vision focusing on the particular nature of the practice, as does

166. Cf. discussion above, chapter 1, section 2.

Menninger's account. No interpretation is right, though some may be wrong; perhaps right and wrong are inappropriate standards, given the character of the activity. The activity is aimed at getting us to feel at home, or feel not at home, in our practices. Since the attitudes each of us hold toward our practices are shaped by our own unique experiences, no one interpretation is likely to work for every person. Justifications of practices as a whole are more or less elaborate visions, and visions either move us, or they don't. They move some but not others.

Each of the justifiers and radical critics we have examined in this chapter looks at legal punishment, but each sees something different. We have found that several thinkers see revenge in punishment, but they disagree about the significance of revenge. Durkheim sees punishment as a manifestation of the social consciousness. If we are persuaded by Durkheim's argument, which hangs together with his much broader theory of social unity, Menninger's view of punishment and revenge will be unpersuasive. Foucault looks at legal punishment and sees something different still—the functioning of a power that disciplines and normalizes. In one passage Foucault suggests to us an image which is intended to help us see things as Foucault sees them. He tells us we "must not forget" that modern investigatory procedures have their origins in the medieval inquisitions.[167] I think Foucault means to link our practices—including scientific and prosecutorial investigations—to an underlying working of power symbolized by the inquisition. Foucault might mean that the linkage between past and present is more tangible than symbolic. His "must not forget" might be more than the invocation of a symbol. But it's not clear what the linkage could be. We have already considered the challenges to the link made between origin and purpose. Nietzsche, whose path Foucault in many ways follows, would, I think, reject the suggestion that because investigatory procedures emerged from the inquisition, all that is good or bad

167. Foucault, *Discipline and Punish*, p. 225.

about the inquisition can similarly be imputed to our existing penal practice.

If Foucault's criticism of punishment is to convince us, we must be able to say yes, the prosecutor or the scientist really is somehow like the medieval inquisitor. We must experience the gaze of the conductor or school teacher or doctor or prison warden as a gaze with coercive designs, rather than as a gaze of loving concern. Our response to Foucault's criticism will depend on whether such a judgment is within us; it will depend, then, on whether, or to what extent, we are at home in our practices. The power of the radical critic is that some who would have said before reading him that they were at home will say afterward that really they aren't. Or he may incite us, get us mad, lead us to take a critical stance from the inside (while he remains outside). For example, some theorists defend capital punishment of convicted murderers as an appropriate expression of society's righteous anger.[168] No longer available to us is another method of expressing our anger: physical torture. Torture would surely vent our indignation. "But we are civilized; we no longer resort to such brutality; capital punishment is more humane—indeed, the convicted criminal suffers no physical pain at all." But it is easy to imagine an effective Foucauldian criticism of this argument, an argument made by those *inside* the practice, committed to punishment but in disagreement about how to inflict it.

If we are at home in our capitalist society, the argument of the Marxists may seem unpersuasive. It depends on a view of society we don't share. The radical criticism Marxists give is much more likely to resonate with those who do not regard themselves as part of a genuine community. To those on the margin, punishment will feel—and be—more like the external and coercive will of the enemy than like their own true will; to such a person, the Marxist view that punishment is a tool

168. Walter Berns, "The Morality of Anger," reprinted in Hugo Bedau, ed., *The Death Penalty in America* (3d ed. Oxford: Oxford University Press, 1982), pp. 333–34.

of the oppressing class may make sense (although well-to-do intellectuals are apt to find the argument more persuasive than would a vagrant).[169]

But as to what punishment *really* is: to expect an answer to this question is to misunderstand what counts as success when justifying practices as a whole. The answer, I am suggesting, lies not "out there" but "in us." The radical critic in effect challenges us to test our commitment to our practices.

Philosophers and theorists often step back to consider why we have our practices at all, just as many of us at times pause and reflect on why we lead the sorts of lives that we do. By saying that these justifiers and critics are engaged in an activity for which there is no clear standard of success, I do not mean to criticize or dismiss them. Many of us are at times uneasy with, not at home in, our practices. At these times it is very important to step back and ask whether we can understand ourselves ever to be at home in them. If we never reflected in this way, we would be stuck with practices we would perhaps be better off without. Moreover, only by stepping back, by standing outside our practices, can the theorist committed to those practices find the standards, the principles, by which she can criticize actions that are part of the actual practice. Only by questioning why we have our practices at all, that is to say, can we offer immanent criticism of our practices.

6. Immanent against Radical Criticism

If the radical critic is successful, he will get us to see our practice in a new light, to see that we are not at home in it. He will knock down our temple. The immanent critic, who derives from an existing practice standards by which to criticize aspects of the practice, is in principle opposed to the project of radical critics. The immanent critic might argue

169. Which merely reflects how vagrants have been too taken in by the bourgeois myth to recognize their own oppression, the Marxist would reply.

that these radical critics, who put us in the confusing and troubling position of living with practices whose justice is denied, leave us homeless. The immanent critic does not claim that our home is perfect or even that it could ever be perfect; rather, she calls us to reflect deeply to see whether or not we are at home in it, despite what the Nay-sayers tell us. The immanent critic calls us to reflect on the costs of assuming the position of radical critic. Radical criticism is appropriate when we are not and cannot be at home in our practices. But as theory that can speak to ordinary people and practitioners, radical criticism is at a disadvantage; its detachment makes for disability. As Michael Walzer says of Foucault, "[W]hen critical distance stretches into infinity, the critical enterprise collapses."[170]

Were I to embrace radical criticism of legal punishment, I'd end this book here. There would be no need to step inside the practice, as eventually we shall do, to consider how we might resolve the questions of for what, whom, and how should we punish. But these questions *are* being asked, and I am sure they still would be asked. Unlike the radical critic, the immanent critic hears and responds to them.

170. Michael Walzer, *The Company of Critics* (New York: Basic Books, 1988), p. 207.

3

Justifications of the Practice: Utilitarian and Retributive

In the previous chapter we considered arguments of radical critics who seem to challenge the whole practice of legal punishment. Now we shall consider theorists whose energies are devoted, not to generating in us skepticism of the practice, but to justifying the practice so that we may be at home in it. As in the last chapter, we will have to be sensitive to the difficulty of justifying practices as a whole: it isn't clear how to tell who is right or wrong about either what the justification for a practice is or whether it is in fact justified.

Philosophers and theorists have long debated why it is that we punish and what principles are involved when we punish. Two competing accounts—utilitarian and retributive—have dominated the discussion, though neither has prevailed.[1] There are distinct versions of both utilitarian and retributive accounts, and sometimes the differences among retributivists seem greater than the differences between some utilitarians and some retributivists. We can, however, describe the two accounts in general terms, as follows: the utilitarian argues

1. Despite what the Supreme Court declared in *Williams v. New York*, 337 U.S. 241, 248 (1949): "Retribution is no longer the dominant objective of the criminal law."

that we should punish only when doing so would augment social utility; the retributivist objects, saying that we must punish those who do wrong, even if doing so diminishes social utility, because justice demands that we punish. Utilitarians are consequentialists, always forward-looking, insisting that an action or a practice is justified only if its future benefits outweigh its future costs.[2] Retributivists are not forward-looking in this way. That an action conforms to a principle of right or justice is, for the retributivist, usually sufficient justification for that action.[3]

Both utilitarians and retributivists claim to give an account of why we punish, of the principle immanent in the existing practice. Both are in a position to be immanent critics: they can use their interpretation of the purpose of and principle immanent in the practice (to augment social utility, to mete out justice) to criticize the actual practice when it diverges from this principle or fails to live up to its purpose. In chapter four, when we step inside the practice and take up, not the justification of the practice as a whole, but particular problems within the practice, we shall see how the theorist's advice to the judge, prosecutor, or sentencing commission member differs depending on the conception the theorist has of why we punish at all. The debate between utilitarians and retributivists matters practically. In chapter four I shall defend a version of retribution. The task of this chapter is to understand both the different retributive accounts of why we punish—this will allow me to distinguish the version I shall defend from others which I find unpersuasive but which most people probably have in mind when thinking about retribution—and various utilitarian versions as well, and to see how the different the-

2. There are utilitarian and nonutilitarian consequentialist theories. For an example of the latter, see Plato, *Protagoras* 324a–b. Cf. Igor Primoratz, *Justifying Legal Punishment* (Atlantic Highlands, N.J.: Humanities Press International, 1989), pp. 9–10.

3. This is not to say that retributivists are never forward-looking. I shall argue that the most persuasive retributive account *is* forward-looking in some sense: see chapter 3, section 3, and chapter 4, section 4, below.

ories clash. We shall examine classic and contemporary accounts, first of committed utilitarians, then of committed retributivists.

1. Utilitarians

When used without care, the label "utilitarian" can apply to anyone, even self-declared opponents of utilitarianism. For example, in the previous chapter we saw that for Marx, punishment is an instrument used by the ruling class to defend itself so that it may maintain itself: punishment, that is, is useful in preserving the ruling class. But Marx is no utilitarian. His aim is not to justify the practice by appealing to principles of utility. Nor should we necessarily call utilitarians all those who, by showing its use for society, *do* mean to justify the practice of legal punishment.[4] Unless I indicate otherwise, I shall reserve the label "utilitarian" for those who justify the practice of legal punishment by appealing to some *principle* of utility or some calculation of net utilities. Probably all practices have or once had a use or function. But whether the practice is justified by some *principle* of utility is another matter.

1.1 Jeremy Bentham

The classic exponent of utilitarianism is Jeremy Bentham, and one of his greatest works lays out a utilitarian justification of legal punishment.[5] For Bentham, the principle of utility is the ground of all moral actions. It is a natural principle that lacks any further ground,[6] and it is not to be questioned: "Systems

4. For example, René Girard or Hans von Hentig—see chapter 2, section 3. Girard argues that legal punishment is a functional equivalent of ritual sacrifice and serves as an outlet for violence, an outlet necessary to the survival of society. Von Hentig argues that punishment serves as a means of selection and security.

5. Jeremy Bentham, *An Introduction to the Principles of Morals and Legislation* (1789; reprinted New York: Hafner Press, 1948). In citing this I refer to Bentham's own chapter/section numbers.

6. Ibid., ch. 1, section 11.

which attempt to question it deal in sounds instead of sense, in caprice instead of reason, in darkness instead of light."[7] For Bentham, our privileged guide is

> that principle which approves or disapproves of every action whatsoever, according to the tendency which it appears to have to augment or diminish the happiness of the party whose interest is in question.[8]

Bentham believes that human beings all, implicitly or explicitly, consent to this principle, which calls on each of us to calculate the pleasures and pains that result from an action we contemplate taking:

> Gross ignorance, they will say, never troubles itself about laws, and passion does not calculate. . . . [But] men calculate, some with less exactness, indeed, some with more: but all men calculate. I would not say, that even a madman does not calculate.[9]

Bentham claims that utilitarian calculation underlies not only human actions in general but legal punishment in particular:

> The business of government is to promote the happiness of the society, by punishing and rewarding. . . . In proportion as an act tends to disturb that happiness, in proportion as the tendency of it is pernicious, will be the demand it creates for punishment.[10]

Bentham maintains that the purpose of punishment is to discourage crimes, which he calls acts of "mischief." A crime produces a "primary mischief," which is sustained by an assignable individual or multitude of individuals, and a "secondary mischief," which is the extension of mischief to un-

7. Ibid., ch. 1, section 1.
8. Ibid., ch. 1, section 2.
9. Ibid., ch. 14, section 28.
10. Ibid., ch. 7, section 1.

assignable individuals or to the whole community.[11] If I am robbed, I sustain primary mischief, and so do family members who care about me or rely on me for support. Society sustains secondary mischief by my being robbed, because the level of "danger" and "alarm" have been increased.[12] The "danger" lies in the suggestion to others of the feasibility of robbing. "Alarm" refers to the increased fear we all suffer from the prospect of being victims of robbery.[13] It is to prevent such mischiefs that we punish. For Bentham, punishment is "an artificial consequence annexed by political authority to an offensive act."[14] We punish in order to augment the total happiness of the community by excluding mischief, which tends to subtract from that happiness.[15]

Punishment is itself a mischief, or evil, since it inflicts pain, and on the principle of utility "it ought only to be admitted in as far as it promises to exclude some greater evil."[16] Punishment does this by reformation, disablement, and compensation, but mainly by "example"—by which Bentham means deterrence.[17] Compensation, or the providing of a "pleasure or satisfaction to the party injured," is not the primary purpose of punishing, because "no such pleasure is ever produced by punishment as can be equivalent to the pain."[18] Bentham sees as primary instead the deterrent function of punishment: "Example is the most important end of all, in proportion as the number of the persons under temptation to offend is to one."[19] Bentham often appeals to the deterrent effects of punishing, for example, in justifying the practice of not punishing retroactively: we cannot deter by punishing someone for an act

11. Ibid., ch. 12, section 3.
12. Ibid., ch. 12, section 5.
13. Ibid., ch. 12, section 8.
14. Ibid., ch. 12, section 36.
15. Ibid., ch. 13, section 1.
16. Ibid., ch. 13, section 2.
17. Ibid., ch. 13, section 2; ch. 15, section 14.
18. Ibid., ch. 13, section 2.
19. Ibid., ch. 13, section 2, note.

he could not have known was mischievous.[20] Similarly, punishing infants or the insane or intoxicated is not warranted, for they could not be deterred.[21]

Bentham, then, gives what is essentially a deterrence-based justification of the infliction of punishment—we inflict punishment to deter future mischief—that is premised on the more general claim that mischief detracts from our happiness, and the increase of happiness should be the ultimate end of all ethical action.[22] Bentham justifies punishment by showing, not that it serves justice, but that it promotes the good.[23]

Once he has established that the purpose of punishment is to yield the good by excluding mischief—which is painful and therefore evil—Bentham argues that we should employ punishment in particular cases only when it lives up to this purpose; he uses his account of the principle immanent in the practice to criticize the actual practice when it diverges from the principle. In Bentham's view, we should punish only when the principle of utility warrants punishment. Therefore, he argues, we should not punish where doing so would be groundless for want of mischief to deter; nor where punishing is inefficacious; nor, as we saw above, "where it cannot act so as to prevent the mischief"; nor where punishing is "unprofitable" or "too expensive"; nor where we could stop the mischief in some other, cheaper way.[24]

20. Cf. ibid., ch. 13, section 7.

21. Ibid., ch. 13, section 9. H. L. A. Hart has sharply criticized this point: "Plainly it is possible that the actual infliction of punishment on the insane or children may deter normal persons" ("Prolegomenon to the Principles of Punishment," in Stanley Grupp, ed., *Theories of Punishment* [Bloomington: Indiana University Press, 1971], p. 369).

22. Bentham defines ethics as "the art of directing men's actions to the production of the greatest possible quantity of happiness" (*Introduction*, ch. 17, section 2).

23. "Now, pleasure is in itself a good; nay, even setting aside immunity from pain, the only good; pain is in itself an evil; and, indeed, without exception, the only evil; or else the words good and evil have no meaning" (ibid., ch. 10, section 10).

24. Ibid., ch. 13, section 3. Bentham infers so many "cases unmeet for punishment" that he runs the risk of undermining his own ar-

Bentham also uses his principle of utility to formulate rules for how we should go about punishing. For example:

> The value of the punishment must not be less in any case than what is sufficient to outweigh that of the profit of the offence.[25]

> The greater the mischief of the offence, the greater is the expense, which it may be worth while to be at, in the way of punishment.[26]

Bentham gives utilitarian accounts of aspects of legal punishment usually justified by retributive principles. For example, he says that punishment should share the characteristic of the offense, for in this way it is an analogy and will be efficacious.[27] Retaliation, therefore, "in the few cases in which it is practicable, and not too expensive, will have one great advantage over every other mode of punishment."[28] Bentham thus gives something approaching a utilitarian justification of the *lex talionis*. Bentham also finds a utilitarian ground for another retributive principle—that we punish in order to express society's moral disapproval of crimes. He suggests that by expressing reprobation for a crime—by using "solemnities"—we can increase the apparent magnitude, without needlessly increasing the cost (level of mischief) of the punishment.[29] Bentham argues, not, as do some retributivists, that we punish in order to condemn; but, rather, that by punishing in a way that expresses

---

gument justifying punishment for its deterrent effect. Most modern deterrence theorists emphasize that if punishment is to deter, the potential criminal must be reasonably certain that his crime will be met with punishment. Bentham would have us factor into our calculation so many variables that no person could know for certain whether in the end the action he weighs would be deemed punishable.

25. Ibid., ch. 14, section 8.
26. Ibid., ch. 14, section 10.
27. Ibid., ch. 15, section 7.
28. Ibid., ch. 15, section 8.
29. Ibid., ch. 15, section 9.

condemnation we can achieve our purpose—more total pleasure and less total pain—at a lower cost.

The retributivist may object to Bentham's justificatory project by claiming that Bentham does not really *justify* punishment—he does not show the justice of the practice; rather, he
gives reasons why punishment is good. The retributivist might
claim that questions of the good are separate from questions
of justice or of what is right, and that before we decide how
to obtain what is good we must know how justice or right
limits what actions we might take to obtain the good.[30] Some
retributivists infer from the utilitarian's emphasis on the good
that the utilitarian ignores questions of right, that in principle
he justifies the manifest injustice of punishing the innocent if
doing so would promote social utility.[31]

Bentham does *not* argue that we should punish an innocent
person, even if doing this would augment the total happiness
of the community.[32] But he does argue that we should not
punish in cases where this would be inefficacious, or unprofitable, or too expensive,[33] and some retributivists would reply
that justice demands that we punish even in such cases. The
dispute will remain obscured unless we make the distinction
between demanding we punish only for an offense (a "negative
retributive principle") and demanding we always punish for
an offense (a "positive retributive principle").[34] At one point

30. A major topic of contemporary moral philosophy is the question of whether the right is prior to the good. Michael Sandel challenges what he takes to be the claim of John Rawls that justice should
have absolute priority over all particular conceptions of the good, by
arguing that we give up the politics of rights for a politics of the
common good. Sandel describes Rawls as a "deontological liberal"
in holding to the moral priority of justice (Sandel, *Liberalism and the
Limits of Justice* [Cambridge: Cambridge University Press, 1982], esp.
Introduction and ch. 1; cf. John Rawls, *A Theory of Justice* [Cam-
bridge, Mass.: Harvard University Press, 1971], esp. chs. 1–2.
31. See chapter 5, section 4.
32. Bentham says explicitly, if not emphatically, that we punish
only in response to "an offensive act" (*Introduction*, ch. 12, section
36; cf. ch. 15, section 25, and ch. 13, section 3).
33. Ibid., ch. 13.
34. Recently such a distinction has been suggested by J. L. Mackie,
Persons and Values (Oxford: Clarendon Press, 1985), pp. 207–8. Cf.

Bentham appears implicitly to assent to the positive retributive principle that we must punish for an offense. Bentham writes that the deterrent effect of punishment

> depends altogether upon the expectation it raises of similar punishment, in future cases of similar delinquency. But this future punishment, it is evident, must always depend upon detection. If then the want of detection is such as must in general appear too improbable to be reckoned upon, the punishment, *though it should be inflicted*, may come to be of no use.[35]

Here Bentham argues that punishment would be useless, and therefore by his own principle ought not to be inflicted, in cases in which punishing would not deter future mischief. However, Bentham, in reflecting on such cases, writes, not that we ought not to punish, but, rather, that punishing would be of no use "though it should be inflicted." This might indicate that he recognizes implicitly that there is some ethical demand (based on utility!) for punishing offenses, regardless of the bearing on utility of actually inflicting punishment in these cases. Of course the "should" here is ambiguous in the English of Bentham's time. It may mean "even were it to be inflicted" rather than "it ought to be inflicted," and so I do not think we should make too much of this point. In one other passage, referring to the accidental punishment of a person innocent of an offense, Bentham uses the phrase "justly punished" to describe the punishment deserved by someone guilty of an offense,[36] thus implicitly acknowledging the negative retributive principle that we may punish only those who commit offenses—justice demands this.

Bentham's position seems to be this: we may justly punish only those guilty of a crime. But though some will say justice demands that we punish all who commit crimes, in some cases

C. L. Ten, "Positive Retributivism," *Social Philosophy and Policy,* vol. 7, no. 2 (Spring 1990), pp. 194–208.
35. Bentham, *Introduction*, ch. 17, section 13, my emphasis.
36. Ibid., ch. 15, section 25.

the principle of utility dictates that we should refrain from carrying out the act of punishment.

Bentham did allow that "lots of punishment" are "variable."[37] Perhaps Bentham's response to the retributivist objection that it is unjust not to punish someone who commits an offense would be to say that we should always punish, but where the punishment we would ordinarily prescribe for a particular crime would be too great a mischief to be justified by utility, we should adjust the punishment to a lower level of mischief, thereby satisfying the demands both of retribution and of utility. The problem with this argument is that it is not consistent with Bentham's principle of utility, which insists that we punish only when punishment will be efficacious. By insisting on this point, Bentham stands opposed to the positive retributive principle that we must punish all offenses. But Bentham himself implicitly accepts the weaker negative retributive principle that we must punish only for an offense, and there is some evidence (though weak) that he might recognize implicitly even the stronger principle which he explicitly opposes.

1.2 Cesare Beccaria

We have seen a tension in Bentham's account between his utilitarianism and his very tentative and implicit acknowledgment of the demands of right or justice. This tension also surfaces in the work of another classic theorist of punishment, Cesare Beccaria. Beccaria is not properly called a utilitarian, for he does not appeal *systematically* to some principle of utility, as does Bentham. But in his famous work *An Essay on Crimes and Punishments*, Beccaria justifies legal punishment, and also its limits, by appealing to the idea of social utility.[38] Beccaria combines elements of both rights-based and utilitar-

37. Ibid., ch. 15, section 2.
38. Cesare Bonesana Beccaria, *An Essay on Crimes and Punishments* (Philadelphia: William P. Farrand and Co., 1809). Beccaria's book was important for its plea for humanity in punishment and for its opposition to the death penalty.

ian theories. Like Hobbes, Beccaria argues that the natural condition of man is a continual state of war, and to escape it we sacrifice part of our liberty in order to enjoy the rest in peace and security; this reservoir of liberty has to be defended, and punishment is the means. Punishment is necessary to restrain passions and preserve our lives.[39] Armed with this principle that we punish to preserve the safety of society, Beccaria goes on to ask of all occasions on which we consider whether to punish, whether punishing is really useful or necessary for the safety or good order of society.[40] As for Bentham, for Beccaria punishment is an evil, and we are to use it only when the principle of social utility dictates that we should:

> The degree of the punishment, and the consequence of a crime, ought to be so contrived as to have the greatest possible effect on others, with the least possible pain to the delinquent—for mankind, by their union, originally intended to subject themselves to the least evils possible.[41]

Beccaria gives essentially a deterrent theory of punishment: the intent of punishment is not to torment or to undo past crime, but to deter future injury to society, and punishment ought to be chosen to maximize its deterrent effect.[42]

But Beccaria's utilitarianism is combined with his rights-based social-contract theory. Beccaria argues that men give up some of their natural liberty and agree to obey the laws and be punished for violating them, only because doing so is necessary to prevent a state of war.[43] Beccaria objects to the death penalty by appealing to his rights-based theory: the sovereign has no right to impose the death penalty, because we never gave to others the right of taking away our lives—in agreeing to the social contract, we each sacrificed only a small

39. Ibid., chs. 1, 4.
40. Ibid., ch. 11.
41. Ibid., ch. 19.
42. Ibid., ch. 12.
43. Ibid., ch. 2.

portion of liberty to the public good. Beccaria, however, also appeals to principles of utility in opposing the death penalty, arguing, for example, that the death penalty does not deter.[44] Hobbes had similarly said that we can never be understood to lay down our right to defend our lives or to resist being wounded, chained, or imprisoned.[45] Hobbes, however, does not argue that the sovereign has no right to punish; his sovereign may do what he pleases, even punish an innocent person without this being an injustice.[46] Hobbes argues, rather, that the sovereign may with right execute me, but I retain the right to try to escape. Unlike Hobbes, Beccaria is not content with declaring the right of the convicted person to try to flee from the executioner, leaving the prisoner a corpse with rights. Beccaria, as we have seen, gives other reasons in arguing against state execution.

Both Bentham and Beccaria justify legal punishment by appealing to some principle of social utility. Both recognize, implicitly or explicitly, limits to their justificatory principle. Bentham implicitly acknowledges that we may justly punish only for a mischievous offense; and Beccaria argues that we may punish only in a way that does not violate the individual rights we carry with us into civil society.

1.3 Richard Posner

The legacy of Bentham and Beccaria has carried over to the present.[47] It is fair to say that utilitarianism is favored among

44. Ibid., ch. 28. Of course, Beccaria does not imply that the murderer should not be punished by some other form of punishment. *Whether* we punish is a separate question from *how* we punish—a point on which I elaborate in the next chapter.

45. Thomas Hobbes, *Leviathan*, ed. Michael Oakeshott (New York: Collier Books, 1962), ch. 21.

46. Ibid., ch. 14.

47. One of the leading utilitarian (in a loose sense) accounts of legal punishment is given by James Q. Wilson, *Thinking About Crime* (rev. ed. New York: Random House, 1985). Wilson opposes the "sociological approach" that tries to trace the causes of crime; he thinks we ought to deter a criminal by increasing the costs and reducing the benefits of crime. Wilson thinks individuals choose the path of

the competing theories and justifications of legal punishment. In this section I shall take as a contemporary example of this legacy the work of Richard Posner, even though for a technical reason Posner distinguishes his account from utilitarianism.[48] Posner takes utilitarianism to the extreme in accounting for many aspects of the practice of legal punishment. His argument is interesting and highly controversial, and because of its extreme character offers us an instructive utilitarian foil to retributive justifications. Also, Posner, with the "law and economics movement" of which he is a leading advocate, has been an influential voice in public policy debates, and so consideration of his argument is particularly appropriate, given our concern ultimately with the application of theory to practice.[49]

---

crime, or at least that we should assume this as a matter of policy (pp. 45–51). In Wilson's view, crime will decline if it becomes less profitable compared to other ways of spending one's time: "Would-be offenders are reasonably rational and respond to their perception of the costs and benefits attached to alternative courses of action" (p. 118).

48. Richard Posner, "An Economic Theory of the Criminal Law," *Columbia Law Review*, vol. 85, no. 6 (October 1985), pp. 1193–1231. The technical reason Posner distinguishes his view from utilitarianism has to do with the difference between the economic concept of value and the moral concept of utility. In Posner's view, we punish to further economic efficiency, and so my stealing a car is wrong because it is an inefficient method of allocating resources or because it moves resources from a more to a less valuable employment. Posner defines value as "a function of willingness to pay." "Since I am unwilling (because unable—but it does not matter why) to pay my neighbor's price for the car, it follows that the car would be less valuable in an economic sense in my hands than in his." Posner adds, "The car might, of course, confer more utility (pleasure, satisfaction) on me than on my neighbor, but there is a difference between utility in a broad utilitarian sense and value in a (perhaps narrow) economic sense, where value is measured by willingness to pay for what is not yours already" (1196, and note 9). One objection to Posner's view is that it doesn't take seriously the discrepancy between willingness and ability to pay. In a (broad) utilitarian theory we can allow that a Stradivarius in the hands of a low-income prodigy is a more valuable allocation of resources than a Stradivarius locked in the vault of a rich investor who can't play a note.

49. See, for example, *New York Times*, October 10, 1988, on the

Posner argues that the criminal law exists to be functionally efficient by serving the goal of wealth maximization. He gives a comprehensive rationale or theory of the criminal law and criminal law doctrine, explaining how this law and doctrine serve to enhance market efficiency. Posner is not obviously engaged in any justificatory activity, at one point saying that he hasn't enough time to consider competing theories:

> If this Article were not already so long, I would go on and compare the economic approach with its principal rival, the "moral" theory of criminal law, which argues that the criminal law should only punish morally blame-worthy conduct. Whatever the normative merits of this approach, I doubt that it is as good a positive theory of criminal law as the economic, since in so many areas conduct is punished that is not blameworthy in the moral sense.[50]

Posner argues that

> [t]he major function of criminal law in a capitalist society is to prevent people from bypassing the system of vol-untary, compensated exchange—the "market," explicit or implicit—in situations where, because transaction costs are low, the market is a more efficient method of allocating resources than forced exchange. . . . Most of the distinctive doctrines of the criminal law can be ex-plained as if the objective of that law were to promote economic efficiency.[51]

---

role of the law and economics movement in the debate about cor-porate penalties.

50. Posner, "An Economic Theory of the Criminal Law," pp. 1230–31.

51. Ibid., p. 1195. We might think that to say, as does Posner, that our practice can be explained "as if" *x were* the principle immanent in it is not to say that *x is* the principle immanent in the practice. But this distinction between "as if" and "is" holds only if we think principles have ontological status. I believe, rather, that to say a prin-ciple inheres in a practice is to make an interpretive claim that reflects not the ontology but one's understanding of a practice.

With this principle—that we punish in order to promote market efficiency—Posner accounts for numerous aspects of the criminal justice system. He accounts for why in most cases we require as a condition for punishment that there be a certain state of mind, or intent, of the accused, a requirement he says is "puzzling to the economist."[52] His answer is that criminal intent identifies "pure coercive transfers," and this is economically important. Where there is intent, we can infer that the criminal invests resources to bring about a wrong, and that the wrong did not emerge accidentally. We should expend the resources needed to punish only where other resources are being expended by the criminal. Otherwise all sorts of serious social costs would be incurred by people avoiding lawful activity in order to prevent the appearance of being engaged in unlawful activity:

> If I take from a restaurant an umbrella that I mistakenly think is mine, I am not a thief; if I know the umbrella is not mine and take it anyway, I am. The economic difference is that in the first case I would have to expend resources to avoid taking the umbrella and the probability of my taking the wrong umbrella is low . . . the risk of overdeterrence through a criminal penalty is great.[53]

Therefore the requirement of intent is justified on economic grounds. Implicit in Posner's account is Bentham's own rule that we should not punish where doing so is unprofitable or too expensive.

Posner's claim that we punish in order to prevent the bypassing of markets may seem plausible in accounting for why we punish those who steal or those who create monopolies.[54] But much of our criminal law is concerned with crimes of

52. Ibid., p. 1221.
53. Ibid.
54. Though retributivists would argue that the thief who steals my property has violated my person, has done something that is morally wrong. The retributivist might appeal to the sense of indignation and the feeling of being violated that one experiences when robbed even of something trivial.

violence. Can Posner's principle account for why we punish the murderer or rapist? Posner thinks so.

> Crimes of passion often bypass implicit markets—for example, in friendship, love, respect . . . less obviously, crimes of passion often bypass explicit markets too. . . . Someone who gets his satisfaction in life from beating up other people, without compensating them, rather than from engaging in trade with them, is thus bypassing explicit markets.[55]

Posner also claims that the rapist bypasses markets: "if [the rapist] spent his time raping rather than dating women he would be bypassing an implicit market."[56] Posner's claim is that having laws against murder and rape is more *efficient* than allowing these "coercive transfers." If we did not punish murderers and rapists and allowed such coercion we

> would create incentives for potential victims to spend heavily on self-protection and for potential aggressors to spend heavily on overcoming the victims' self-protective efforts. All this spending would yield little if any net social product.[57]

Posner realizes how perverse his argument sounds and at least pauses to acknowledge that of course "rape is a bad thing." He says his point is that "economic analysis need not break down in the force of such apparently noneconomic phenomena as rape."[58] At this point his argument is far removed from not only a justification but also an explanation of some aspects of legal punishment—he gives a rationale which is not in the least bit persuasive as an account of the reasons we punish crimes of violence.

55. Posner, "An Economic Theory of the Criminal Law," p. 1197. One of Posner's examples "of a lawful market alternative to battery" is professional boxing (p. 1198, note 12).
56. Ibid., p. 1198.
57. Ibid.
58. Ibid., p. 1199.

Posner's account is troubling, especially to the retributivist. Posner sees the criminal justice system as an instrument we can fine-tune to promote economic efficiency. For example, he claims that we adjust the probability of apprehension (for example, by increasing or reducing the number of police) with the length of sentence, in order to approach an efficient use of resources. When we make more arrests and reduce the length of sentence, we trade litigation and pre-trial detention costs for prison costs.[59] The retributivist objects to the very idea of adjusting the level of arrest—it is unfair that who gets apprehended and punished depends on the decision of policy-makers concerned with economic efficiency. Posner acknowledges this claim that selective enforcement of laws "creates ex post inequality among offenders,"[60] but he sees nothing wrong with this. The criminal justice system, in his view, is like a lottery, and lotteries aren't unfair:

> Nor is it correct that while real lotteries are voluntary the criminal justice "lottery" is not. The criminal justice['s] is voluntary: you keep out of it by not committing crimes.[61]

But those holding to the positive retributive principle find selective enforcement unacceptable, not merely because it is unfair, but because it is premised on the mistaken view that it is not inherently wrong to allow some crimes to go unpunished.

When we turn to the contemporary utilitarian-retributive debate (chapter five, section 4), we shall see that an important retributive objection to utilitarianism is that in principle the utilitarian, who justifies an action on the basis of whether it augments social utility, is committed to punishing an innocent person if the principle of utility recommends doing so. None of the utilitarians we have discussed justifies the punishing of

59. Ibid., p. 1213.
60. Ibid.
61. Ibid.

an innocent person for the sake of augmenting social utility. Even Bentham implicitly rules this out. But neither Bentham nor Posner accepts the claim that seems fundamental to the retributivist position: that there are such things as wrongs deserving of punishment. For Posner, the reason we call (and ought to call) certain activities wrongs, or crimes, is that they bypass the market and therefore promote economic inefficiencies; for Bentham, the reason is that these activities, or mischiefs, take away from society's total happiness. Each holds that the reason we have the whole practice of legal punishment is to augment social utility, however understood; each is therefore willing in particular cases to say "don't punish," if the principle each sees underlying the practice as a whole determines that we should not punish. Each explicitly rejects the positive retributive principle that we must always punish for an offense, a principle to which many retributivists hold. We might think that one is not a retributivist *unless* one holds to this principle. Our task now is to see just what it means to be a retributivist.

2. Retributive Justifications of Legal Punishment

There is a great deal of confusion about precisely what it is to be a retributivist. One of today's leading retributivists himself does not think "retribution" is a helpful term: Andrew von Hirsch notes that the *O.E.D.* definition of "retribution" as "return of evil" and the declaration in the 1972 Model Sentencing Act that "sentencing should not be based upon revenge and retribution" illustrate how retribution is often confused with vindictiveness.[62] The report of the Royal Commission on Capital Punishment clarifies how retribution can be understood differently:

> Discussion of the principle of retribution is apt to be confused because the word is not always used in the same

62. Andrew von Hirsch, *Doing Justice* (Westford, Mass.: Northeastern University Press, 1986), pp. 45–46.

sense. Sometimes it is intended to mean vengeance, sometimes reprobation. In the first sense the idea is that of satisfaction by the State of a wronged individual's desire to be avenged; in the second it is that of the State's marking its disapproval of the breaking of its laws by a punishment proportionate to the gravity of the offense.[63]

Ambiguity exists not only in the meaning of "retribution" but in the burdens of a retributive justification of punishment. Some think that the amount of punishment need not be a just amount for the punishment to be justified on retributive grounds.[64] Others argue that any deviation from the just amount of punishment is unjust and therefore state punishment, which can never hope to mete out punishment with such precision, cannot be justified by an appeal to the principle of retribution.[65] From our previous discussion we know of other possible criteria for being a retributivist. To be a retributivist, must I hold that we must punish all wrongs (positive principle), or merely that we must never punish an innocent person (negative principle)? To be a retributivist, must I hold that we punish only morally blameworthy conduct? Our task in this section is to answer these questions by examining various accounts of punishment commonly regarded as retributive.

We shall consider four sorts of retributive accounts, which I shall refer to as (1) revenge (associated by some with the *lex talionis*); (2) condemnation; (3) deontological theories; and (4) just deserts.

63. *Report of the Royal Commission on Capital Punishment* (London: H.M.S.O., 1953), pp. 17–18, cited in Joel Feinberg, "The Expressive Function of Punishment," in his *Doing and Deserving: Essays in the Theory of Responsibility* (Princeton: Princeton University Press, 1970), p. 101.

64. C. W. K. Mundle, "Punishment and Desert," in Grupp, ed., *Theories of Punishment*, p. 66.

65. A. C. Ewing, *The Morality of Punishment* (London: Kegan Paul, 1929), cited in Mundle, "Punishment and Desert," pp. 66–67.

2.1 Revenge

Oliver Wendell Holmes wrote that retribution is "only vengeance in disguise."[66] Most of us, when we hear someone declare that we ought to punish for the sake of retribution, associate retribution with revenge or retaliation (which we wrongly conflate).[67] We think of the biblical expression of the *lex talionis*:

> And if any mischief follow, then thou shalt give life for life, eye for eye, tooth for tooth.[68]

> Breach for breach, eye for eye, tooth for tooth: as he hath caused a blemish in a man, so shall it be done to him again.[69]

We have been taught to resist the urge to retaliate:

> Ye have heard that it hath been said, An eye for an eye, and a tooth for a tooth: But I say unto you, That ye resist not evil: but whosoever shall smite thee on thy right cheek, turn to him the other also.[70]

Christianity has denounced retaliation, and, consequently, in the minds of many, retributive accounts of punishment. Of course, many of us do not easily heed Christ's words. We hardly need the survey research of social scientists (though

66. Oliver Wendell Holmes, *The Common Law* (Boston: Little, Brown, 1923), p. 45.
67. The justice of retaliation, or *lex talionis*, was deeply entrenched in the moral sensibilities of the Greeks and other archaic societies: see Gregory Vlastos, "Socrates' Contribution to the Greek Sense of Justice," *Archaiognosia*, vol. 1, no. 2 (1980), pp. 304ff. It was thought of as repayment, and the metaphor of paying back a debt was often used to characterize this sense of justice. Revenge is different, measuring punishment by the feelings of the victim.
68. *Exodus* 21:24.
69. *Leviticus* 25:20.
70. *Matthew* 5:38–39.

the data are available) to tell us that revenge is an urge deeply seated in us.[71]

The law of the *talio*, or of retaliation, is not necessarily connected to the idea of revenge. To see punishment as revenge is to focus on the motivations of the punisher, whereas the *lex talionis* is a law of equivalence that dictates what punishment is commensurate with the crime; it is not a theory of motivation. *Both* the *talio* and the view that we punish to avenge have been discredited by most modern retributivists.

Retributivists needn't commit to the *lex talionis*. One of the most famous and important retributivists, Hegel, is sharply critical of the *lex talionis*, using Blackstone's example to make his point: "an eye for an eye, a tooth for a tooth—and then you can go on to suppose that the criminal has only one eye or no teeth."[72] In any case, what amount of punishment we inflict is one question; why we punish is another. No retributivist of repute takes the *lex talionis* as the justification for punishing at all. One modern retributivist, Joel Feinberg, calls "incoherent" the version of retributive theory that insists "that the ultimate justifying purpose of punishment is to match off moral gravity and pain, to give each offender exactly that amount of pain the evil of his offense calls for, on the alleged principle of justice that the wicked should suffer pain in exact proportion to their turpitude."[73]

Nor need retributivists commit to the idea that we punish to avenge. The most persuasive retributivists distinguish their

71. See, for example, the very dated but still interesting study by F. C. Sharp and M. C. Otto, "A Study of the Popular Attitude Towards Retributive Punishment," *International Journal of Ethics*, vol. 20, no. 3 (April 1910). The authors conclude that revenge is deeply built into the values of those surveyed, "contrary to traditional Christian ethics."

72. G. W. F. Hegel, *Philosophy of Right*, trans. T. M. Knox (1821; London: Oxford University Press, 1952), par. 101, Remark, p. 72. Hegel opposes, not the idea that the severity of the punishment we inflict should be equivalent in value to the severity of the crime, but only the strict equivalence established by the *lex talionis*.

73. Feinberg, *Doing and Deserving*, p. 116.

view from revenge theories of punishment. For Hegel, the judge who oversees legal punishment is not an avenger. Whereas revenge can be arbitrary and further the wrong, the judge of a rational modern state must be "cold, heartless, and have only the interests of the law," and this presupposes the education or cultivation (*Bildung*) of a modern state.[74] Hegel says that the word *Gerechtigkeit* (justice) comes from the word *Rache* (revenge) and that in uncivilized (*ungebildeten*) states justice is revenge,[75] but in rational modern states revenge is too contingent and arbitrary and subjective to serve justice or right.[76] In an earlier work Hegel explains that if we rely on the sufferer or his next of kin to punish, then right is mixed with arbitrariness; legal punishment depends, rather, on a third party.[77]

Revenge, as Hegel describes it, is subjective; it derives from feelings of anger and resentment within an individual. Not all retributivists, however, take anger to be a subjective measure residing only within individuals. Walter Berns defends punishment as an expression of anger, but the anger he means resides not merely within the hurt victim but within society. The anger Berns thinks punishment expresses is a righteous anger, an anger "somehow connected with justice." For Berns, this anger is not "a selfish indulgence," but "may more accurately be called a profound caring for others."[78]

74. G. W. F. Hegel, *Vorlesungen über Rechtsphilosophie* (1818–1831), 4 vols., ed. Karl-Heinz Ilting (Stuttgart-Bad Canstatt: Friedrich Fromman, 1973), vol. 4, p. 556.
75. Ibid., vol. 4, p. 294.
76. G. W. F. Hegel, *Grundlinien der Philosophie des Rechts*, in Hegel, *Werke in zwanzig Bänden*, ed. Eva Moldenhauer and Karl Michel (Frankfurt am Main: Suhrkamp, 1970), vol. 7, par. 102.
77. G. W. F. Hegel, *Philosophische Propaedeutik*, in Hegel, *Werke*, vol. 4, part 1, par. 21.
78. Walter Berns, "The Morality of Anger," in Hugo Bedau, ed., *The Death Penalty in America* (Oxford: Oxford University Press, 1982), pp. 334–35. See also Stanley Brubaker, "Can Liberals Punish?" *American Political Science Review*, vol. 82, no. 3 (September 1988): "[P]unishment expresses and satisfies righteous anger" (p. 825).

Anger is expressed or manifested on those occasions when someone has acted in a manner that is thought to be unjust, and one of its origins is the opinion that men are responsible, and should be responsible. . . . We can become angry with an inanimate object (the door we run into and then kick in return) only by foolishly attributing responsibility to it, and we cannot do that for long, which is why we do not think of returning later to revenge ourselves on the door. . . . Anger recognizes that only men have the capacity to be moral beings and, in so doing, acknowledges the dignity of human beings.[79]

By punishing to vent our anger,

we demonstrate that there are laws that bind men across generations as well as across (and within) nations, that we are not simply isolated individuals, each pursuing his selfish interests and connected with others by a mere contract to live and let live.[80]

Berns tends to speak of punishment as justified "revenge." But rather than see his retributivism as a revenge theory, I think we should invoke a distinction Hegel suggests, between revenge, which is subjective and appeals to an individual's feelings of hurt; and righteous anger, which reflects a social judgment. We can then understand Berns's retributivism as advocating, not the vindictive satisfaction of personal *desires* to avenge, desires of the sort that fuel violently destructive blood feuds, but, rather, the satisfaction of the *demands* of justice and right. Berns's retributivism, then, more properly belongs to the next variety of retributive theories we shall consider.

Some may think our lust for revenge explains why we punish. But few retributivists of repute take revenge to be the principle we use to guide us in our practice, and most reject the view that the purpose of punishment in a modern state is

79. Ibid., p. 334.
80. Ibid.

to satisfy the desire to avenge. Retribution as revenge is not a compelling account of legal punishment, and it is not the version of retributivism I shall defend.

2.2 Condemnation

According to a second version of retributivism, we do not punish to deter, incapacitate, reform, or satisfy a private desire for vengeance; rather, punishment is justified as an expression of society's condemnation of the offensive act.

Henry Hart emphasizes the condemnatory or reprobative function of punishment in answering the question he poses of what is the distinctive function of criminal (as opposed to other) law. Some utilitarians argue that there is no essential difference in purpose between criminal and tort law; to Richard Posner, for example, the only time there is a justification for invoking criminal rather than civil remedies is when the latter "bump up against a solvency limitation."[81] Hart claims there *is* an essential difference; in his view, criminal law, unlike other law, reflects "the judgment of community condemnation which accompanies and justifies its imposition."[82] Whereas a tort is an injury to a private person, a violation only of private law, a crime is an affront to the social morality articulated in criminal or public law. Crime is

> conduct which, if duly shown to have taken place, will incur a formal and solemn pronouncement of the moral condemnation of the community.[83]

Hart concurs with the view that

> The essence of punishment for moral delinquency lies in the criminal conviction itself. One may lose more money on the stock market than in a court-room; a prisoner of war camp may well provide a harsher environ-

81. Posner, "An Economic Theory of the Criminal Law," p. 1204.
82. Henry M. Hart, Jr., "The Aims of the Criminal Law," *Law and Contemporary Problems*, vol. 23 (Summer 1958), p. 404.
83. Ibid., p. 405.

ment than a state prison. . . . It is the expression of the community's hatred, fear, or contempt for the convict which alone characterizes physical hardship as punishment.[84]

Hart takes issue with humanitarian theories that see treatment as the aim of punishment, for such theories fail to see that the essential aim of punishment is to express condemnation:

Today "treatment" has become a fashionable euphemism for the older, ugly word ["punishment"]. This bowdlerizing of the Constitution and of conventional speech may serve a useful purpose in discouraging unduly harsh sentences and emphasizing that punishment is not an end in itself. But to the extent that it dissociates the treatment of criminals from the social condemnation of their conduct which is implicit in their conviction, there is danger that it will confuse thought and do a disservice.[85]

Like all the utilitarians we considered, Hart uses his account of the essential aim of punishment to criticize the existing practice. He says his thesis is "that a sanction which ineradicably imparts blame, both traditionally and in most of its current applications, is misused when it is thus applied to conduct which is not blameworthy."[86]

Joel Feinberg also emphasizes the reprobative function of legal punishment. Feinberg contends that

[p]unishment is a conventional device for the expression of attitudes of resentment and indignation, and of judg-

84. George K. Gardner, "Bailey v. Richardson and the Constitution of the United States," *Boston University Law Review*, vol. 33 (1953), p. 193, cited by Hart, "The Aims of the Criminal Law," p. 405. Neither Hart nor Feinberg, who also cites this passage, observes that contempt and fear are separate reasons for punishing. Fear may motivate the utilitarian more than contempt or hatred does. Punishing in order to condemn is similar in some ways, different in others, from punishing out of revenge, but the equation of condemnation with the expression of hatred or contempt tends to stress only the similarities.
85. Hart, "The Aims of the Criminal Law," p. 405.
86. Ibid., p. 405, note 13.

ments of disapproval and reprobation, on the part either
of the punishing authority himself or of those "in whose
name" the punishment is inflicted. Punishment, in short,
has a *symbolic significance* largely missing from other
kinds of penalties.[87]

But Feinberg distinguishes his view from Hart's. Hart suggests
that condemnation alone may count as punishment, even absent the added consequences of unpleasant physical pain:

> [O]therwise, it would be necessary to think of a convicted
> criminal as going unpunished if the imposition or exe-
> cution of his sentence is suspended.[88]

For Feinberg, what makes something legal punishment is its
reprobative force *and* its being "hard treatment."[89] Whereas
Hart suggests that hard treatment is a distinct and nonessential
feature of punishment—the convicted criminal whose sentence is suspended is still punished, still stigmatized—Feinberg
points out that in some cases it is only the actual infliction of
hard treatment that constitutes punishment: "it does not always happen that the convicted prisoner is first solemnly condemned and then subjected to unpleasant physical treatment."[90] Hard treatment itself brings shame and ignominy and
stigma: "[C]ertain forms of hard treatment have become the
conventional symbols of public reprobation."[91]

The condemnation theory of punishment might seem to be
nothing but a theory of *public* vengeance. Feinberg suggests
that punishment is in part "a symbolic way of getting back at
the criminal, of expressing a kind of vindictive resentment."[92]
But in the condemnation theory, punishment also expresses
judgments of community disapproval, which needn't be motivated by resentment or even by anger. The condemnation

87. Feinberg, "The Expressive Function of Punishment," p. 98.
88. Hart, "The Aims of the Criminal Law," p. 405.
89. Feinberg, "The Expressive Function of Punishment," p. 98.
90. Ibid., p. 99.
91. Ibid., p. 100.
92. Ibid.

theory is not merely a theory of public vengeance, though it is that as well. It understands legal punishment to serve other purposes besides the venting of public anger, purposes which are distinct also from those declared by the utilitarian. One purpose of punishment, in Feinberg's view, that presupposes its expressive function is the authoritative disavowal of what was done. Another is the vindication of the law:

> A statute honored mainly in the breach begins to lose its character as law, unless, as we say, it is *vindicated* (emphatically reaffirmed); and clearly the way to do this (indeed the only way) is to punish those who violate it.[93]

The retributivist notes that only by punishing do we affirm right. Unless we punish a wrong, it will be held to be valid.[94] Hegel suggests that to have a law the violation of which is to be called a "wrong" or "crime" *logically* requires punishing those who violate it:

> [P]unishment, as we have seen, is only crime made manifest; i.e. is the second half which necessarily presupposes the first. Prima facie, the objection to retribution is that it looks like something immoral, i.e. like revenge, and that thus it may pass for something personal. Yet it is not something personal, but the concept itself, which carries out retribution.[95]

> [I]t would be impossible for society to leave a crime unpunished, since that would be to posit it as right.[96]

A third function of punishment noted by Feinberg is the absolution of others: "Quite often the absolution of an accused hangs as much in the balance at a criminal trial as the inculpation of the accused." Of course, the state could do this job

93. Ibid., p. 104.
94. Hegel, *Philosophy of Right*, par. 99.
95. Ibid., par. 101 addition.
96. Ibid., par. 218 addition.

without punishing, "but when it speaks by punishing, its message is loud and sure of getting across."[97]

All of these functions are nonutilitarian reasons for punishing. They are forward-looking or consequential in some sense, in that they appeal to some future good, be it the vindication of right, absolution of someone wrongly accused, or whatever good we associate with the venting of righteous anger; but it is not on the basis of a calculation of utilities, pleasures and pains, or effects on economic efficiency that they are regarded as good reasons. They are moral or ethical reasons for punishing that presuppose that the purpose of legal punishment is to express public condemnation of certain actions we call crimes.[98]

2.3 Deontological Retributive Theories

It might be surprising to hear a retributive theory characterized as forward-looking or consequential, for retributivism is usually characterized as nonconsequential, as "deontic." According to one commentator, "[r]etributivism is a deontological theory, different in its logical behaviour from its teleological counterpart."[99]

> A teleological theory would consider the punishment as the means to some good, either general or individual. But the obligation laid upon us by "This is a just punishment" asserts the independent moral value of the punishment itself, considered apart from, and even to the frustration of, some prudential value to be derived from its effects. . . . In a teleological theory we may ask of each action in a sequence "why?" until we reach an answer that is considered prudentially sufficient. . . . In a deon-

97. Feinberg, "The Expressive Function of Punishment," p. 105.
98. In chapter 4, section 4, I shall defend a consequentialist retributivism. The sense in which this retributivism is consequentialist is rather weak; but it is nevertheless forward-looking enough to be distinguished from the deontic theory we shall consider in the next section.
99. Mary MacKenzie, *Plato on Punishment* (Berkeley: University of California Press, 1981), p. 29.

tological theory, on the other hand, "why?" questions terminate in a judgment which is considered to be morally sufficient—maybe from an intuitionist point of view.[100]

In this view, where retributivism is seen as a deontological theory that is mutually exclusive of teleological theories, the retributivist insists that we punish, not for any consequences, such as to deter future crimes, or to reform or incapacitate the criminal, but, rather, for the sake of punishing, because punishing is in itself just or right—regardless of the good it may yield.

Does anyone hold such a view? If anyone does, it is Kant,[101] and it is to his views about legal punishment that we now turn.

The conventional understanding of Kant is that he is a retributivist who opposes all utilitarian justifications of punishment, instead holding that we punish only because justice demands this.[102] I shall argue that this understanding gets Kant wrong. Kant, it is true, rejects consequentialism in thinking about moral actions, but Kant also thinks law and morality are separate spheres: the justification for a moral action has a different character from the justification for a legal action. Kant's theory of *legal* punishment is not deontological.

In his *Lectures on Ethics*, Kant distinguishes moral from pragmatic laws; the latter comprise statute and common law.[103] Pragmatic laws constrain actions related to other peo-

100. Ibid.
101. MacKenzie, who makes the claim that retributivism is a deontological, not a teleological, theory, thinks Kant's is the paradigm of a deontological theory of punishment (ibid., p. 29, note 39).
102. For example, Mitchell Franklin says that in Kant's view it is not justified to punish in order to deter ("The Contribution of Hegel, Beccaria, Holbach and Livingston to General Theory of Criminal Responsibility," in *Philosophical Perspectives on Punishment*, ed. Edward H. Madden, Rollo Handy, and Marvin Farber (Springfield: Charles C. Thomas, 1968), p. 102. See also Brubaker, "Can Liberals Punish?" p. 826.
103. Immanuel Kant, *Lectures on Ethics*, trans. Louis Infield (New York: Harper Torchbooks, 1963).

ple; unlike moral laws, they demand compliance regardless of one's moral disposition.[104] Whereas pragmatic laws are made by governments, moral laws have no author.[105] Kant then makes the following distinction, which seems so often ignored: the punishment imposed by a being who is guided by moral standards is retributive,[106] but punishment for the violation of (pragmatic) law is imposed to deter or reform:

> All punishments imposed by sovereigns and governments are pragmatic. They are designed either to correct or to make an example.[107]

> Ruling authorities do not punish because a crime has been committed, but in order that crimes should not be committed.[108]

Kant thinks that the risk of punishment should not be our ground for avoiding evil deeds. We use rewards and punishment in order to make up for our lack of morality,[109] not to inspire moral action. Kant thinks it is wrong to use the threat of punishment to inspire moral action, but that through punishment man acquires the habit of doing good deeds.[110]

In his often neglected essay *On the Old Saw: That May Be Right in Theory But It Won't Work in Practice,* Kant gives a hypothetical example in which he appeals implicitly to deterrence as the justification for legal (but not moral) punishment.[111] Kant supposes that one man on a life raft pushes the other off to save his own life. Kant says the man does not have a duty to save his own life; rather, he has an unconditional

104. Ibid., p. 48.
105. Ibid., pp. 51–52.
106. Ibid., p. 55.
107. Ibid.
108. Ibid., p. 56.
109. Ibid.
110. Ibid., p. 57.
111. Immanuel Kant, *On the Old Saw: That May Be Right in Theory But It Won't Work in Practice,* trans. E. B. Ashton (Philadelphia: University of Pennsylvania Press, 1974).

duty not to take the life of someone else who is not causing the danger threatening his life. (Kant does not consider the objection that the other man, by consuming what food and drink are available, is indirectly causing a danger to the life of the first.) But, in a footnote, Kant defends "law professors" as

> quite consistent in making legal allowance for such emergency acts. For the authorities can't attach any punishment to this injunction, because that punishment would have to be death, and it would be an absurd law that threatened death to one who refuses to die voluntarily in a dangerous situation.[112]

Kant's reasoning is that state laws, by threatening us with sanctions, are intended to prevent us from acting in certain ways. The point of these laws is to deter. Consequently, a law that imposes a punishment that could not deter the action the law proscribes is absurd. In his *Metaphysics of Ethics* Kant repeats the lifeboat example and makes the further distinction that the rescued person's killing is not inculpable (*unsträflich*) but is impunible (*unstrafbar*).[113] Here it is clear how important is Kant's separation of law (*Legalität*—whether an action accords with a law without further consideration of motivations) and morality (*Moralität*). Legal duty is external duty, whereas ethical or moral duty is internal duty.[114] Legal duty binds by force or coercion (*Zwang*).[115] In the lifeboat example there is a moral, not a legal, duty not to kill the other person. The res-

112. Ibid., p. 68, note.
113. Immanuel Kant, *Metaphysik der Sitten*, in Kant, *Werke in Sechs Bänden*, vol. 4, ed. Wilhelm Weischedel (1798; reprinted Darmstadt: Wissenschaftliche Buchgesellschaft, 1963), AB41–42.
114. Ibid., AB15.
115. Ibid., AB16. Kant also makes the distinction between *recht* and *gerecht* (right and justice). He says that legal action is either *gerecht* or *ungerecht*; moral action is either *recht* or *unrecht* (AB23). Kant's distinction is not unlike Hobbes's distinction between injustice and iniquity: Hobbes writes in *Leviathan* that the sovereign can do no injustice, but he may commit iniquity (ch. 18).

cued person is to be morally condemned but not legally punished.

Kant's theory of legal punishment does not rule out utilitarian considerations, but does it make sense to call his a retributive theory? If so, it is not because Kant thinks we punish to avenge: "[T]o insist on one's right beyond what is necessary for its defence is to become revengeful . . . such desire for vengeance is vicious."[116] There are other reasons why we call Kant a retributivist. Kant holds to the principle of equality in punishing. In the *Metaphysics of Ethics* Kant writes: "[W]hatever undeserved evil you inflict on someone, you do to yourself. . . . [I]f you strike him, you strike yourself; if you kill him, you kill yourself."[117] Kant draws the conclusion that my action should literally be turned back on me—if I kill another, I should be killed.[118] Kant thus adopts a version of the *lex talionis*, though he carefully distinguishes this view from one of private revenge.[119] He also allows that the principle of equality can be valid, if not in the letter, then in its effect; for example, justice can require a nobleman to apologize publicly if he insults someone of lower class, since a fine would have no impact on him.[120]

Another reason we call Kant a retributivist is that he insists that a person may be punished only because he has committed a crime, and not for any other purpose:

> The criminal must be found to be worthy of punishment [*strafbar*], before it is to be thought that from his punishment some use for himself or his fellow citizens can be drawn.[121]

Kant argues that we cannot punish someone merely to achieve some further good; he opposes, for example, a proposal to

116. Kant, *Lectures on Ethics*, p. 214.
117. Kant, *Metaphysik der Sitten*, A197–98, B227–28.
118. Ibid., A199, B229.
119. Ibid.
120. Ibid., A198, B228.
121. Ibid., A196–97; B226–27.

have a person on death row participate in dangerous experiments that could yield beneficial results.[122] Underlying Kant's position is the view that human beings should not be treated only as a means to some end:

> Now I say that man, and in general every rational being, exists as an end in himself, not merely as a means for arbitrary use by this or that will: he must in all his actions, whether they are directed to himself or to other rational beings, always be viewed at the same time as an end.[123]

This aspect of Kant's theory has been emphasized by other retributivists who oppose what are called humanitarian theories of punishment. A humanitarian theory is a variation of utilitarian theory that advocates therapy and treatment, not punishment.[124] Karl Menninger, whose views we considered in chapter two, gives such a theory. For Menninger, punishment is nothing but the infliction of pain and suffering; punishment is inhumane and does no good, and our resources would be better spent reforming the criminal who has done "so human a thing."[125]

The retributivist objection to this seemingly benign position is best expressed by Hegel. In his early *Propaedeutik* Hegel opposes those who think the state should help people by treating or reforming them even though the person being helped

122. Ibid. We might ask Kant why he thinks it is wrong to conduct medical experiments on a prisoner, so long as her imprisonment is deserved. In that case she is not being treated *merely* as a means.

123. Immanuel Kant, *Groundwork of the Metaphysic of Morals*, trans. H. J. Paton (New York: Harper Torchbooks, 1964), p. 95; see in general pp. 95–103.

124. MacKenzie, *Plato on Punishment*, prefers to distinguish humanitarian from utilitarian theories. For her, both are teleological theories, but for utilitarians the end for which punishment is the means is a general good, whereas for humanitarians it is an individual good.

125. Another example of a humanitarian theory is that of Norval Morris and Donald Buckle, "The Humanitarian Theory of Punishment: A Reply to C. S. Lewis," in Grupp, ed., *Theories of Punishment*, pp. 309–16.

does not consent: "To help someone in need, that person must will that I help him, that I still will regard and treat him as equal."[126] Why? Hegel, drawing on Kant's idea of human beings as ends in themselves, explains in his later *Philosophy of Right*:

> Punishment is regarded as containing the criminal's right and hence by being punished he is honoured as a rational being. He does not receive this due of honour unless the concept and measure of his punishment are derived from his own act. Still less does he receive it if he is treated either as a harmful animal who has to be made harmless, or with a view to deterring and reforming him.[127]

Kant's theory of *legal* punishment is not deontological, since for him a legal punishment is not justified that could not deter wrongs. But the theory is retributive, inasmuch as Kant holds to the negative retributive principle that we must punish for no other reason than that a wrong was committed. (However, we've seen that Bentham, a classic utilitarian, also holds to this principle.) Kant gives another hypothetical example, one that appeals to the stronger, positive retributive principle: on an island where all the people were to depart the next day, forever dissolving and dispersing the community, the last murderer in jail would have to have his execution carried out before the diaspora, because justice demands this. Kant is a retributivist because he holds that justice must prevail, "else a people is doomed."[128] The utilitarians we have discussed would contend that in such cases, where punishment could not possibly be justified by the principle of utility, we should refrain from punishing. On this point Kant and the utilitarians disagree.

At this point we might be puzzled by Kant's views, for the diaspora example is difficult to reconcile with Kant's other

126. Hegel, *Philosophische Propaedeutik*, part 2, par. 66.
127. Hegel, *Philosophy of Right*, par. 100, Remark.
128. Kant, *Metaphysik der Sitten*, A196–97, B226–27. Note how Kant's formulation is consequentialist but not utilitarian.

hypothetical example, that of the lifeboat, whose point is that legal punishment must deter. With the diaspora example Kant claims that desert is a necessary and sufficient condition for punishment. Kant chose the diaspora example precisely because it presents a case in which we must punish even though there is no conceivable basis in utility for doing so. How could Kant claim both that the person on the lifeboat who kills the other need not be punished, because doing so would not provide any deterrent benefit, and that a murderer who could pose no possible future threat to his society must nevertheless be punished? I think a plausible answer is that in the lifeboat example Kant is saying, not that we should not punish a wrong where doing so would be ineffective, but, rather, that the killing should not be regarded as a criminal action, or wrong. Kant can with consistency hold both that we should not call a crime any action that could not be deterred by the threat of legal punishment, and that we must punish crimes even when doing so would not augment social utility.

A deontological theory that insisted we punish even though such punishing would lead to society's destruction would not be very attractive. Retributivists are typically characterized, rather unflatteringly, as nonconsequentialists, as only backward-looking. It is true that for the retributivist the fact that a crime occurred in the past is a compelling reason for punishing. But, as our discussion in this chapter should make clear, one can be a retributivist and still take consequences into account. Both the revenge and the condemnation version of retribution make reference to a future good: the satisfaction of personal desires, or the vindication of right. Utilitarianism is not the only theory that is forward-looking in any degree.[129]

129. Justice Thurgood Marshall wrote in *Gregg v. Georgia*, 428 U.S. 153 (1976): "The . . . contentions that society's expression of moral outrage through the imposition of the death penalty pre-empts the citizens from taking the law into its own hands and reinforces moral values—are not retributive in the purest sense. They are essentially utilitarian in that they portray the death penalty as valuable because of its beneficial results." Marshall, apparently of the understanding that retributivism *means* being oblivious to consequences

The retributivist position I shall defend is not strictly deontological; it recognizes the importance of justice and right, but
is unwilling to insist on justice "though the world perish."

2.4 Just Deserts

A final version of retributivism follows in the footsteps of Kant,
up to a point. In this version, desert is a necessary but not
sufficient condition for legal punishment. A leading advocate
of this view is Andrew von Hirsch, who chaired the Committee
for the Study of Incarceration, which clarified the conception
of punishment as just deserts.

Von Hirsch argues that utilitarianism alone cannot justify
a person's punishment—desert is needed: "While deterrence
accounts for why punishment is socially useful, desert is necessary to explain why that utility may justly be pursued at the
offender's expense."[130] In the just deserts theory, desert and
deterrence are both essential features of punishment. That
someone deserves punishment does not imply that we must
punish him, only that we have reason to do so. Because there
are moral reasons not to punish, deterrence is needed to "tip
the scales back in favor of penal sanction."[131] The argument,
then, is that: (1) committing a criminal act deserves punishment, and desert is a prima facie justification; (2) there is a
moral obligation not to add deliberately to the amount of human suffering, which punishment does, and this overrides the
case for punishment in (1). Deterrence disposes of the coun-

---

and that arguing for something on the basis of its good consequences
means one is a utilitarian, winds up labeling as utilitarian what clearly
is a retributive position. Marshall could have avoided stretching utilitarianism so far had he seen that to be a utilitarian one must justify
an action or practice by appealing to a calculation of net utilities.
On the rejection of the simple dichotomy of "deontological" and
"consequentialist" (that is, that one must be either one or the other),
see Charles Larmore, *Patterns of Moral Complexity* (Cambridge: Cambridge University Press, 1987), esp. p. xi.
   130. Von Hirsch, *Doing Justice*, p. 51.
   131. Ibid., p. 54.

tervailing argument in (2), and so (1) stands.[132] Since we may safely assume that in some situations (3) will not outweigh (2), von Hirsch's version of retributivism as just deserts holds to the weaker negative retributive principle that demands merely that we punish only for an offense, not to the positive retributive principle that we punish all offenses.

Von Hirsch overlooks an important point, one that is central to the retributive position I shall defend: we can be committed always to punishing for an offense, for retributive reasons, without being committed to inflicting punishment in a certain way. In his argument above, von Hirsch acknowledges a moral demand to express condemnation (to punish), but also recognizes a moral objection against the infliction of pain or suffering (punishment). But not all legal punishment inflicts pain or suffering. The retributivism I shall defend insists that we punish when punishment is deserved, but recognizes that how (or how much) we punish is a separate matter. This is the position Hegel takes: "[T]he only interest present is that something be actually done [i.e., *that* we punish] . . . no matter how."[133] Von Hirsch fails to take into account that we can with consistency insist always on punishing, for retributive reasons, and insist that the *way* we punish be justified on utilitarian grounds.

In the theory of retribution as just deserts the idea of desert is used to account for why it is morally permissible to punish certain individuals, but in itself it does not account sufficiently for why we are justified in having a practice that punishes those who deserve punishment.[134] But not everyone accepts even

132. Ibid.
133. Hegel, *Philosophy of Right*, par. 214, Remark; cf. par. 214, Z.
134. David Dolinko has recently distinguished the "moral justification" of punishment—an account of why it is morally legitimate to punish, or of by what right we may punish—from the "rational justification" of punishment—an account of for what reason we punish at all. Dolinko notes that we can agree that there are reasons for punishing without agreeing that it's morally legitimate to punish, and vice versa ("Some Thoughts About Retributivism," *Ethics*, vol. 101, no. 3 [April 1991], pp. 539–40).

the idea that because a person has committed a crime, it is, on the theory of just deserts, morally permissible to punish him. Consider the (true) story of Leroy Strachan. Mr. Strachan was recently arrested in New York City by two Miami police officers. He was wanted for the murder of a police officer in Miami forty-three years previously. In the intervening years Mr. Strachan, now a sixty-one-year-old Harlem resident, married, raised three children, and operated an elevator in SoHo for twenty-one years. The manager of the building where Mr. Strachan worked describes Mr. Strachan as "a very good worker who never had a problem." Since the incident forty-three years previously, Mr. Strachan had not been arrested for any offense. When the Miami police officers confronted him with the crime, Mr. Strachan confessed. If extradited to Florida and convicted, he could face the death penalty.[135] According to the theory of just deserts, should Mr. Strachan be punished?

Some retributivists would insist, for various reasons, that Mr. Strachan, if convicted, does deserve punishment. Von Hirsch, however, on the basis of the theory he lays out, would probably be committed to opposing his punishment, since in this case punishment is unlikely to have much of either a general or a specific deterrent effect.[136] So, too, would another theorist who offers a more sophisticated version of the theory of just deserts. In James Griffin's view, retribution as just desert is premised on the idea that desert is a reason for action, but not one that necessarily trumps other reasons. Griffin argues that merit (or desert) is not a *moral* reason for action or a criterion for moral right and wrong, but it is a reason for action: "The element of appropriateness itself constitutes a reason."[137] Griffin means that it is appropriate to express admiration for one who merits it—to admire only on utilitarian

135. *New York Times*, February 17, 1990.
136. General deterrence refers to the effect on members of society in general; specific deterrence, to the effect punishment would have on Mr. Strachan.
137. James Griffin, *Well-Being: Its Meaning, Measurement, and Moral Importance* (Oxford: Clarendon Press, 1986), p. 259.

grounds would not really be to admire; but your merit does not give you a right to receive, nor impose a duty on me to express, my admiration. Griffin then takes the case of punishment—a case of demerit rather than merit—and comes to somewhat different conclusions. Griffin argues that your demerit is a moral reason for punishing you, but only under what he calls the "repentance view."[138] What you did was morally wrong, so I have a moral reason to punish you, but "my response to your wrongdoing is appropriate only when, and to the extent that, it contributes to your going through the . . . process: perception, guilt, and repentance."[139]

Griffin distinguishes the repentance view from what he calls the atonement view, which he dismisses. In the atonement view, my *act* of demerit needs to be punished; but the problem with this view is that "if I change, I should want [people] to respond now to the person I am now."[140] If I *have* changed, neither deterrence nor retaliation seems appropriate.[141] Griffin identifies Kant with the atonement view and suggests that Kant, who does not want to deny to a person the dignity of being morally accountable, fails to see that

> the atonement view is not the only way to show respect for persons. . . . If anything, it is the repentance view, in which a person is given more weight than an act, that shows respect for persons.[142]

In Griffin's view, then, the only desert-based moral reason for punishing me is, not to atone for the wrong I've done, but to

138. Ibid., p. 270.
139. Ibid., p. 272. Griffin's argument, then, seems to be: if you commit a wrong, then you deserve to be punished—we have a moral reason to punish you. But it's appropriate to give you what you deserve only if doing so will get you to repent. In other words, the moral reason for punishment is weighed against the criterion of appropriateness. In this argument is the same sort of utilitarian weighing we find in von Hirsch's argument. The Kantian would question Griffin's invocation of the criterion of appropriateness.
140. Ibid., p. 268.
141. Ibid., p. 269.
142. Ibid.

make me repent.[143] And "if the wrongdoer is an exceptional moral agent who spontaneously repents and reforms, there is virtually no place for punishment."[144] On the other hand,

> if he is an adult who still needs to learn but resists the lesson, then maybe punishment would teach the seriousness of wrongdoing where words alone would fail. If he is someone who cannot learn no matter what the lesson, then punishment has no place as a response to the person that we are dealing with.[145]

Griffin, then, suggests a reason not to punish Mr. Strachan.[146]

Although Griffin speaks of desert as a moral reason for punishing, in his view it amounts only to a necessary but not sufficient condition for punishing. Griffin comes to a conclusion similar to von Hirsch's, although some would call his view humanitarian and von Hirsch's utilitarian, since for Griffin the sufficient condition for punishment is moral improvement of the individual, whereas for von Hirsch it is the improvement of society that results from deterrence.

The retributivists who focus on just deserts seem to give in to utilitarianism, and we might ask whether there is any essential difference between the two sorts of justifications. Retributivism in the version of just deserts holds only to the weaker, negative retributive principle, that we punish only those who are guilty of a crime. Neither von Hirsch nor Griffin expresses Kant's demand that we must punish when we have reason to punish. None of the utilitarians we discussed denies that desert is a necessary condition for punishment. In the theory of punishment as just desert, utilitarianism and retributivism blur.[147]

143. Ibid., pp. 270, 272.
144. Ibid., pp. 270–71.
145. Ibid., p. 271.
146. It's unclear whether Griffin himself would apply his argument in this way. He clearly states that his argument applies to *moral* punishment. Other considerations may enter for him when thinking about *legal* punishment.
147. Cf. Dolinko, "Some Thoughts About Retributivism," p. 543.

3. Deciding between the Utilitarian and Retributive Accounts

We have examined both utilitarian and retributive theories of why we legally punish at all. We have seen that some theorists who claim to be retributivists sound very much like utilitarians. Before deciding between the two accounts, we must first establish what version of retributivism we shall hold up to utilitarianism, and see whether we indeed need to choose between the two.

From our account of theorists commonly called retributivists it is clear that there is no distinct set of criteria the satisfaction of which is essential for meriting that label. Some retributivists (von Hirsch, Griffin) hold only to the weak, negative retributive principle that declares we may punish only for an offense. This principle is an offshoot of the Kantian demand that we treat each person as an end and not merely as a means—we may not punish for any reason other than desert (demerit). But we have seen that utilitarians also hold to the negative retributive principle (*how* they can do so consistently will be taken up in chapter 5, where we consider rule-utilitarianism). Other retributivists (Kant) hold to the positive retributive principle that we must punish all offenses, a demand the former group of retributivists reject. Some retributivists (Feinberg, Kant, Hegel) insist that we punish the act to vindicate right, and others (Griffin) insist that we punish the person and, therefore, that if the person changes, punishment is no longer justified on retributive grounds. Some retributivists (Henry Hart, Feinberg) insist that we legally punish only morally blameworthy conduct, and it is this demand that constitutes their retributivism. Kant rejects this demand.

The retributivist label, then, might not seem particularly useful, for the differences on particular issues among some retributivists may seem greater than the differences between some retributivists and some utilitarians. Still, there are features of some of the theories commonly called retributive that clearly distinguish them from utilitarian theories and that, I believe, persuasively articulate an ideal immanent in the practice of legal punishment. I refer to the insistence that we punish to express condemnation of an act society regards as blameworthy, to mete out just deserts, and to vindicate right. These purposes are inextricably connected. We might say they amount to different articulations of one single purpose: that we punish for justice.

This version of retribution insists that we punish to mete out just deserts, but it does not commit to the nonconsequential Kantian version of (moral) retribution that insists we punish for the sake of justice "though the world perish." Yet, in holding that we have a compelling reason for punishing that is independent of what the consequences are either to the sum of individual utilities or to economic efficiency, it *is* opposed to the utilitarian accounts we considered. Although it draws on the idea von Hirsch emphasizes, that we punish to mete out just deserts, it insists, contrary to von Hirsch's compromise retributivism, that we must punish to vindicate right even if a utilitarian calculation would determine that we shouldn't punish. This retributive position is not oblivious to consequences. It need not insist that we send people to prison even if it were the case that prisons were "schools for crime" and doing so would lead to more crime. The theory insists only that we express our condemnation *in some way*, for if we do not declare that a criminal did something that was wrong, then "right" and "wrong" have no meaning.

The retributivist position that we punish to express righteous anger, mete out just deserts, and vindicate right points to an ideal of justice I believe is immanent in the practice of legal punishment, but an ideal which sometimes gets lost in the shadows of our institutions. It is the version of retributivism I shall defend. But how does one go about defending a justification for legal punishment? How does one justify the claim that the retributive and not the utilitarian theory is the best account of why we punish?

One approach is to appeal to what "punishment" means in ordinary language. Consider the following exchange:

Reb: "The essence of punishment is that it is deserved. Punishment is punitive. It is a response to a wrong, an expression of our condemnation. If it's not deserved, it's not punishment but something else."

Ute: "Sometimes we punish people not because it's deserved, but to deter future crime or to incapacitate the criminal. For example, we will inflict additional punishment on a repeat offender because we believe he poses a future threat to society. This is part of our practice, and it counts as punishment."

Reb: "The moment the prison sentence that is deserved expires, the repeat offender who remains in chains as a future threat is no longer being punished. If it's not for a past wrong then it's not punishment but some other practice, and we might even give it a different name, say, 'telishment.' "[148]

Ute: "I bet this 'telishment' that's not really 'punishment' sure would feel like punishment to the poor man!"

Reb: "Well, telishment feels a lot like punishment, but sometimes so does illness. What makes something punishment is not that it hurts, but that it's deserved. Spanking a child is punishment, but not merely because it hurts; for we also call it punishment when a teacher sends a naughty pupil to the back of the room and makes her wear a duncecap. This is no doubt painful, but no physical pain has been inflicted. Sometimes punishment embarrasses, sometimes it physically hurts. Sometimes neither is the result. Being given extra homework or receiving a parking fine needn't embarrass or hurt; and the death penalty doesn't embarrass and can be quite painless. All of these things are punishment, because they are responses to an action regarded as wrong or blameworthy, as deserving of condemnation."

In this exchange Reb is pointing to the *punitive* character of punishment, a character implied by our use of the word in

148. The idea of "telishment" comes from John Rawls, "Two Concepts of Rules," in Michael Bayles, *Contemporary Utilitarianism* (Gloucester, Mass.: Peter Smith, 1978), pp. 59–98.

ordinary language. The retributivist, like Reb, can appeal to the meaning of the word "punish" and the concept of punishment in arguing that we punish to express condemnation of those who deserve it. We shall see in chapter 5 that Reb's appeal to ordinary language is not entirely convincing, that there is no single *essence* of punishment: we *do* call it punishment when we inflict pain or hurt or stigmatization on those who, by Reb's standards, might not deserve it. Mistaken punishment of innocent persons, punishment of those who did not intend to commit a wrong, and extended punishment of repeat offenders are all still called "punishment"—and *are* punishment—even though we might not think the pain, hurt, or stigmatization is deserved. A defense of retributivism based on linguistic intuition won't be enough to satisfy everyone (or even myself).

The immanent critic insists that the ideals according to which she criticizes actual practice derive from the practice. Both the utilitarian and the retributive immanent critics claim they have adduced the principle immanent in the practice. Ultimately, to decide who is right, we have to *look at* the practice, see what is done and what principle best makes sense of what is done. We must ask whether the utilitarian or the retributivist ideal better fits the practice. In looking at actual practice, we shall see aspects that accord with both principles; the retributivist, for example, will find many instances where the ideal of condemning blameworthy actions and vindicating right is not what is being done by practitioners. In such cases, the retributivist might have to stick to his ideal in the face of contrary facts and argue that such instances, although part of actual practice, go against the best conception of what it means to punish. In deciding between retributivist and utilitarian accounts, then, we are deciding which ideal better accords, on the whole, with the purpose of the practice, with the concept of punishment, and even with the meaning of the word "punish."[149] Ultimately, to decide between the two ac-

---

149. We've seen that when justifying a practice as a whole, there

counts we must step inside the practice and see what is done. This we shall do in the following chapter.

---

are no clear standards for what counts as success (chapter 1, section 2). In chapter 5, section 2, we shall consider more explicitly how we decide among competing justifications of a practice. On my view that practices as a whole lack absolute grounds and on my commitment to nonfoundationalism, see also chapter 1, note 26, chapter 2, note 95, and chapter 5, note 2.

4

Retributive Immanent Criticism of Legal Punishment

1. An Internal, Discriminating Approach to Legal Punishment

In this chapter we take an internal approach to legal punishment. Having attained some distance in reflecting upon theories of why we have the practice at all, now we step inside the practice, both to see whether the utilitarian or the retributive theory offers the better account of the actual practice and to criticize aspects of, or resolve issues raised by, the practice by appealing to the principle we think underlies the practice as a whole.

Legal punishment is a complex practice. It consists of various subpractices: the making of laws the violation of which merits punishment; the arrest and pre-trial detention of those suspected of violating those laws—what I call clutching; the determination of a defendant's guilt; the sentencing of the criminal; and the infliction of punishment upon the convicted criminal. The first subpractice, lawmaking, produces laws that apply to "persons," who, if thought to have violated a law, become "suspects" to be clutched; once clutched, suspects become "defendants," who go through a process to determine whether they are guilty; if convicted, the defendant becomes a "criminal" and, if sentenced to prison, a "convict." Each subpractice has meaning by virtue of its being part of the practice as a whole, just as the meaning of each term—person, suspect, defendant, criminal, convict—is determined by contrasting it with the others: to be a defendant is no longer to be a suspect or a mere person; to be a convict presupposes that one is a criminal, which presupposes that one was a defendant and, before that, a suspect. These facts reveal the continuity among subpractices; they indicate how the subpractices are connected as parts of a single, complex practice. In the previous chapters we were concerned with the general question, why punish? In this chapter our concern is with particular questions that emerge within each subpractice: why punish *for this*? (lawmaking subpractice); on what grounds *may you* judge and punish me? (clutching); why punish *her* for this (determination of guilt); why punish her *in this way*? (sentencing and infliction of punishment). Take a typical response a philosopher might give to the general question:

> *Philosopher:* "Why punish? We shouldn't! The practice of punishing people is absurd. Inflicting harm on others is barbaric, something we should be above. Perhaps this moral evil would be justified if it did some good, but in fact punishment only makes worse the problem it is supposed to solve. When we send criminals to prison not only do we breed resentment in them, but the prisoner makes new connections and learns new techniques from other criminals so that he comes out a better criminal. At the very least, to punish is to violate the principle that you should not try to treat a patient unless you know you can make him better."

Our philosopher is making some very good points, but is he giving a convincing argument against legal punishment? Not at all. He is making what is essentially an objection to ways we inflict punishment (pain, prison). If he draws the conclusion that we should no longer have the practice of legal punishment, then we can expect (and I suspect we will agree with) the following response:

> *Practitioner:* "So what are you suggesting? That we let people commit rape and murder and theft? That we decriminalize all dangerous and morally reprehensible actions? That we abolish the police, shut down our criminal courts, jails, and prisons, and disband our parole boards? You may choose to live in such a society, but not me; it is you who proposes the absurdity."

Our practitioner is pointing out that inflicting punishment, against which the philosopher speaks, is but one part of the practice of legal punishment, and that there is something terribly wrong with the suggestion that we abolish the whole practice because of objections to one part of it.

In this chapter we shall take a *discriminating approach* to the practice of legal punishment. We shall make explicit what is implicit in the argument of our practitioner: that the infliction of pain is one aspect, or subpractice, of the practice of legal punishment, and that to justify, or criticize, a subpractice is not to justify, or criticize, the whole practice. Our philosopher may be right that our manner of inflicting punishment is barbaric and that we should stop it. But does it follow that because we go about punishing in an objectionable way, we should abolish the practice of legal punishment—criminal laws, police, jury system, parole boards included? If our philosopher is not intending radically to challenge our whole system of law and enforcement mechanisms, but instead is expressing moral outrage against inflicting pain, then by taking a discriminating approach we can eliminate the pointless argument between our philosopher and our practitioner, and perhaps get them working together on the genuine problem of how we should inflict punishment, as opposed to whether in general we should punish.

2. Immanent Criticism in a Complex Practice

The immanent critic is committed to applying the principles and standards immanent in a practice, or an interpretation of the purpose of the practice, in justifying or criticizing actions that are part of the practice. The immanent critic believes that the way we ought to practice is determined by the way we do practice, by the practice's implicit ideals. The immanent critic can be critical because actual practice often diverges from these implicit principles and ideals. The immanent critic of legal punishment answers particular questions, such as what should be made criminal, or to what standard of accountability we should hold defendants, or what level of sentencing is appropriate, by appealing to the purpose of the practice as a whole. The immanent critic still has to confront the radical critic, who holds that the practice is bad root and branch and who therefore is not satisfied with appeals to principles immanent in the practice, as well as those who don't see a need to act according to any principles and prefer simply to muddle through.[1] But with this done, it might seem that the immanent critic, with principle in hand, could offer clear guidance to prosecutors, trial judges, sentencing commission members, and other practitioners. It would be nice if things were so simple. But once we accept immanent criticism as a plausible and even an attractive strategy, we still must face three further complications to applying immanent criticism to legal punishment, complications which we shall address in both this and the following chapter.

First, we disagree about the principles immanent in the practice of legal punishment. As we've seen in the previous chapter, some think the principle is utility, others, retribution,

---

1. In chapter 2 I responded to the objections of the radical critic; I don't explicitly address the latter objection, primarily because to do so adequately would entail considerable discussion of the nature of the objection, and this would take us in a direction I don't feel compelled to go, given that my concern is with justifications or reasoned arguments.

and both sides' claims have merit. Some features of the actual practice accord unambiguously only with the principle of utility, and others only with the principle of retribution. As we shall see in this chapter, the immanent critic committed to one principle (utility or retribution) will recommend an action precisely the opposite of that recommended by the immanent critic committed to the other. In this chapter I shall defend the retributive account, arguing that it better captures the ideals at the core of punishment and provides the standards by which we can criticize the actual practice. At first my defense can rest only on an appeal to ordinary language, to our understanding of the word "punish" and the concept of punishment—an appeal outlined in the previous chapter.[2] Eventually I shall defend retributivism by arguing that it better accounts for more of the features of the practice of legal punishment, but this I can do only as we take up more and more of these features.[3] In the final chapter, however, I shall suggest that legal punishment is an essentially contested practice: *both* utility and retribution are principles immanent in the practice. In the final chapter I shall have to consider the problem of how one can be a retributive (or, for that matter, a utilitarian) immanent critic of a practice acknowledged to be essentially contested.

A second difficulty with immanent criticism of legal punishment arises because legal punishment is a complex practice, consisting of subpractices some of which we might want

2. See chapter 3, section 3.
3. The twofold task of this chapter—both defending retribution as the best account of why we do punish, and using the retributive principle to criticize the practice immanently—creates some logistical difficulties. How can I *use* retribution to criticize or justify features of the practice, while at the same time *defend* retribution by arguing that it accounts better for why we punish? If the features of actual practice are the "data" that (dis)confirm the retributive theory, how can I use the theory to discredit some of the data (i.e., by arguing that some features ought not to be part of the practice)? To avoid this catch–22, we have to see that immanent criticism is dialectical: it depends on a give and take between the theory and the "data" for which the theory is supposed to account.

to regard as autonomous, as practices in their own right. When justifying an action within a subpractice of legal punishment that can also be regarded as its own practice, it's not clear by which principle we should be guided: that immanent in legal punishment as a whole, or that immanent in the autonomous subpractice. Take plea-bargaining, where the prosecutor offers a defendant a reduced sentence in exchange for a plea of guilty to a lesser offense. Negotiated pleas are part of the practice of legal punishment. As we shall see, the retributivist might argue that they shouldn't be, on the ground that plea-bargaining is inconsistent with the principle immanent in legal punishment. But suppose we regard plea-bargaining as a practice in its own right. Then we could be immanent critics of plea-bargaining, addressing ourselves to this particular practice. The immanent critic of plea-bargaining could study its history, try to understand the ways in which it has been defended—and then criticize particular corrupt uses of it, without reference to the principles immanent in legal punishment. The argument that plea-bargaining is an autonomous practice and should be regarded as unconnected to the larger practice of legal punishment is, however, unconvincing, especially since the prosecutor or defense attorney who initiates the plea and the judge who approves it are choosing an alternative that might be precluding the actions which the principles immanent in legal punishment oblige them to undertake.

But although I don't think we should regard plea-bargaining as an autonomous practice, there *are* two subpractices of legal punishment that we can more plausibly regard as practices in their own right: lawmaking and clutching. Lawmaking is an essential component of legal punishment. But neither the utilitarian nor the retributive account of why we punish can account for all aspects of lawmaking or determine how we should resolve the controversial issue of what the scope of the criminal law should be. The utilitarian principle would have us threaten with the penal sanction the doers of all actions that create mischief or disutility sufficient to outweigh the costs of imposing the penal sanction. The retributive principle (that is, the version I defended at the end of chapter 3, that declares we punish to express condemnation, mete out just deserts, and vindicate right) would have us punish all actions that society regards as worthy of its condemnation. The utilitarian and the retributivist might agree for the most part about what these actions should be, insofar as actions that create mischief or disutility (murder, rape, larceny) are actions which incite society's righteous anger and of which society disapproves.[4] But neither principle is sufficient to guide lawmakers. Most of us believe there are limits to what the state may legitimately proscribe or demand of us. There are many actions (or inactions) that diminish social utility, or of which we disapprove, but which we don't think it's any business of the state to prevent (or require)—for example, spitting on the sidewalk, cursing in public, not showering for weeks, being dull, arriving late for an appointment. Lawmaking is part of legal punishment, but it is also a practice in its own right, with principles at work concerning the proper limits of state interference.

Clutching—which itself includes many sub-practices, such as the stop-and-frisk, surveillance, arrest, and pre-trial detention—also is both part of the complex practice of legal punishment and a practice (or complex practice) in its own right. The institution that clutches, the police, is used for other purposes besides legal punishment, such as crowd control, traffic regulation, and instilling a sense of security and respect for authority. Clutching might be seen as a practice in its own right. We have a police force not merely to punish, but to provide a sense of security to society. Many political scientists have noted that it is not the purpose of the criminal justice system, or of the police, strictly to enforce every law on the books, but, rather, to do what is necessary to maintain social order.[5] Someone might defend having a police force that, with-

4. Of course, the retributivist's sense of indignation is not a sense of dismay at not maximizing utility.

5. On the social-functional role of the police, see, for example, William K. Muir, Jr., *Police: Streetcorner Politicians* (Chicago: University of Chicago Press, 1977); and J. Q. Wilson, *Thinking About Crime* (rev. ed. New York: Random House, 1985), part 2.

out punishing offenders, physically prevents people from doing certain actions. However, we might think that by linking clutching to legal punishment we gain insight into why we clutch at all.

A third complication facing the theorist who seeks to resolve the particular problems facing those inside the practice of legal punishment is that in addition to utility and retribution, other principles are immanent in the practice, and there are values external to the practice that conflict with those underlying the practice, but which we, a people with *many* practices, nevertheless cherish. For example, we value the prosecution of the guilty, but we don't require some family members to testify against each other because we also value family unity; nor, in many cases, do we allow evidence obtained in violation of an individual's rights, as established in the Fourth Amendment to the Constitution, to be used even though it could help convict a guilty person, because in addition to valuing the capture and punishment of wrongdoers, we value individual liberty.

I argue that theory matters to our problem-ridden practitioners; in trying to resolve our practical problems it matters what our conception is of the purpose of and principle(s) underlying the practice of legal punishment as a whole. But to say theory matters is not to say the task of doing theory will be easy; it certainly won't be with a practice as complex and conflicting as legal punishment.

3. Practical Problems of Legal Punishment

We convict a murderer, sentence her to death, and execute her. If someone asks, "Why punish?" in this specific context he might mean any of the following sorts of questions: why punish *for murder*? Why punish *this* murderer? Why punish *by execution*? Our philosopher, not preoccupied with the practical concerns of those working within the criminal justice system, grapples, not with these specific variants, but, rather, with the more general question: why inflict punishment at all? Many Marxists who challenge the practice of punishing are also concerned with none of the specific variants listed above, but, rather, with a further variant: why may *the state* punish this murderer? In this section we shall discriminate among these variations of the general question "Why punish?" each of which is associated with a distinct subpractice, as we consider several of the problems practitioners of legal punishment confront.

3.1 Lawmaking

Even those who have doubts about punishing in general would probably approve of punishing murder if anything is to be punished. But why? The retributivist would say, because murder is morally reprehensible. Perhaps. But then do we determine what we should criminalize by applying the *principle* that we punish for actions violating society's moral values? Many would disagree, arguing that the law should be neutral, that we should not "legislate morality." We may all agree that murder is wrong, but with respect to many actions (consensual homosexual sodomy, abortion, the use of drugs or alcohol, gambling, adultery) we disagree about what is right or wrong. Who should decide? Many would say, not the state.

But, then, by what principle *do* we determine that murder is a crime? Opposed to the retributive principle that we punish actions violating society's conception of right stand utilitarians who argue that the actions we make crimes detract from social utility; the principle of utility determines what we criminalize.[6] Of course, utilitarians might disagree about how to apply their principle. Currently there is a debate over whether to legalize crack, the cocaine-based drug. Some argue we should, because legalization would eliminate the profit motive for drug-dealing gangs, thereby reducing gang-related violence; social utility would be augmented by not making crack use a crime. Others invoke the same utilitarian principle to argue that we should

6. There are other possibilities as well for why we punish murder. Prominent among them are custom and Scripture. But from the person who appeals to custom we can continue to demand a justification for the custom.

not legalize crack, on the grounds that if we did, society would be worse off—legalization "would likely produce a surge of new addiction—and a health catastrophe."[7]

This dispute among utilitarians could be resolved, in theory, by empirical studies that convincingly predicted the consequences of legalizing crack. But there are retributivists who don't care about these consequences. If it's wrong to use crack, whoever uses crack must be punished. To the retributivist, debating about social consequences misses the point of why we punish at all. Henry Hart articulates the retributivist position on lawmaking:

> In its conventional and traditional applications, a criminal conviction carries with it an ineradicable connotation of moral condemnation and personal guilt. Society makes an essentially parasitic, and hence illegitimate, use of this instrument when it uses it as a means of deterrence of conduct which is morally neutral.[8]

Hart suggests that we should make criminal *only* actions that are morally blameworthy, because only then do we act in accordance with the purpose of the practice.

In practice, though, we do criminalize morally neutral actions solely for the sake of deterrence. We punish for "strict liability offenses," or actions regarded as a crime even though the perpetrator did not intend to do wrong:

> where one deals with others and his mere negligence may be dangerous to them, as in selling diseased food or poison, the policy of the law may, *in order to stimulate proper care*, require the punishment of the negligent person though he be ignorant of the noxious character of what he sells.[9]

7. See *New York Times*, December 13, 14, 15, 1989, editorial and op-ed pages.
8. Henry M. Hart, Jr., "The Aims of the Criminal Law," *Law and Contemporary Problems*, vol. 23 (Summer 1958), p. 424.
9. *U.S. v. Balint*, 258 U.S. 250 (1922), my emphasis.

Or take the case of the "cyberpunk," who enters computer networks without authorization. Unauthorized entry into a computer network is not widely considered immoral—the novelty of this phenomenon makes it very difficult to judge by conventional standards of right and wrong. But "cyberpunks" are a nuisance to other computer users. One prosecutor was quoted as saying: "It's a question of deterrence. We have to do something or we'll have hundreds of these yo-yos."[10]

To the retributivist, such facts about the practice need not deny the ideal; the retributivist immanent critic argues that whenever the law is used merely to deter action that is morally neutral, the law is misapplied and should be changed. Penalties or regulatory fines might be appropriate, a civil suit may be in order, but to punish the "cyberpunk" or the violator of a "strict-liability" offense is to employ punishment wrongly, for punishment must be deserved and must express society's righteous anger.

Retribution and utilitarianism are important guiding principles in determining for which actions it is appropriate to invoke penal measures. But, as we have seen above, the question of the proper scope of the criminal law is too complicated to be determined solely by appeal to the principle(s) immanent in legal punishment. To answer the question of what we should criminalize, it's not enough even to decide the difficult question of whether we punish for utilitarian or retributive reasons. What I call the subpractice of lawmaking can be understood as part of the practice of legal punishment, so that we might think the principle(s) underlying the whole practice should guide us in this subpractice; but lawmaking can also be seen as a practice in its own right. The state which makes criminal laws exists to do other things as well; and so in thinking about the problem of what we should criminalize, we need to consider the purpose, not only of legal punishment, but also of the state. Our concern is not merely, for what should we punish? but, more generally, what are the limits of state action?

10. *New York Times*, November 26, 1988, p. A7.

with what actions does the state have a right to interfere at all? Resolving the utilitarian-retributive debate won't necessarily help us with *this* issue. We need a theory of right(s)—perhaps a liberal theory of individual rights that establishes the boundaries of individuals which the state may not legitimately cross; or a theory of public right, or legal moralism, that rejects the idea that the rights of autonomous individuals are sovereign and sees as legitimate a far more expansive criminal law.

The most comprehensive treatment of the problem of the proper scope of the criminal law is provided in Joel Feinberg's four-volume work, *The Moral Limits of the Criminal Law*.[11] Feinberg considers four possible principles that set conditions for when it is legitimate to limit liberty: (1) the "harm to others" principle warrants punishment of a person who does something to harm another and is a principle of which Feinberg says "no responsible theorist denies the validity";[12] (2) the "offense to others" principle warrants punishment of those who hurt or offend others; (3) the "harm to self" principle justifies limiting the liberty of persons who would otherwise harm themselves; and (4) the "legal moralism" principle warrants punishment of those engaging in inherently immoral conduct regardless of its harm to anyone.[13] Filling out these principles is a monumental task: what counts as a harm, as opposed to an offense?[14] as *causing* a harm?[15] how do we determine what conduct is "inherently immoral"?

11. Joel Feinberg, *The Moral Limits of the Criminal Law*, 4 vols. (New York: Oxford University Press, 1984–1988).

12. Feinberg, *Moral Limits*, vol. 1 (*Harm to Others*), p. 14.

13. John Stuart Mill adopted the first principle, that the state may punish only to prevent harm to others (*On Liberty*, ed. Gertrude Himmelfarb [Harmondsworth, England: Penguin Classics, 1985], pp. 68–69). As Feinberg notes, there are passages where Mill suggests he holds also to the more expansive offense principle (Feinberg, *Moral Limits*, vol. 1, p. 14; cf. Mill, *On Liberty*, ch. 5, par. 7).

14. Feinberg defines a harm as both a setback to interest (this accounts for why, when my favorite football team has lost, I can't say it has harmed me in a legal sense—my interests have not been set back, for I had no real stake in the team); and a violation of a

This is not the place to address these and related questions. The point I want to make is that the issues concerning law-making are very complicated and can't be entirely resolved merely by agreeing on the purpose of the practice of legal punishment. We might think that the retributivist would commit to principle 4, and therefore that the retributive account of punishment *does* claim to determine what actions we should make criminal. But retributivists needn't be legal moralists; the version of retributivism that I have argued is most persuasive claims only that the reason we punish lawbreakers is to express condemnation, mete out just deserts, and vindicate right. It does not follow from, though it is consistent with, this principle that all actions of which society disapproves ought to be legally punished. Retributivists can also hold to a liberal principle that respects the autonomy of individuals and that limits which actions deserving condemnation the state might legitimately proscribe; indeed, such respect for autonomy is the basis of some retributivists' criticism of utilitarian theories of punishment. As we've seen, both Kant and Hegel criticize utilitarians for using punishment as a threat and thus failing to respect human beings as rational agents.[16]

Utilitarianism is also not a rich enough theory to determine which of the four principles should limit the scope of the criminal law. The utilitarian might believe herself able to determine whether we should punish drunkenness, drug use, gambling, adultery, discreet prostitution, or live sex shows, but whether it is legitimate for punishment in these cases to take the form of *state* punishment (as opposed to other forms of social pressure, or even state *regulation*) depends on what we

---

person's right (this accounts for why a person who doesn't return my love has not harmed me in a legal sense, for I have no right to be loved back). Cf. *Moral Limits*, vol. 1, chs. 1, 3.

15. Complications arise when there are concurrent or intervening causes. Another problem is whether my failure to act to save someone should be seen as "causing" a harm (Feinberg, *Moral Limits*, vol. 1, chs. 3, 4).

16. See my discussion, chapter 3, section 2.3.

think the proper role of the state is in our lives, on which of Feinberg's four principles we think determine the proper moral limits of the criminal law. If, like some classical liberals, we think we join the state merely to protect our person and property, then we may think the state may legitimately invoke its police power only to limit actions that victimize a person or property.[17] But if we think the liberal account of why we join the state is empty, perhaps even that the state is not something we join at all, then we may give to the law far broader scope than does the liberal.

3.2 Clutching

The first requirement for legal punishment is the existence of laws; the next stage of the process is the apprehension of suspects, which may involve, among other things, a police investigation, surveillance, a stop-and-frisk, arrest, and pre-trial detention. Various issues emerge at this stage of the process, the stage I call "clutching."[18] Clutching is a metaphor that suggests a taking hold by some power. Clutching need not always be seen as a Leviathan's jaws closing on its victim; it

17. Richard Epstein, for example, drawing on Locke's view that the chief end of joining political society is to preserve our property, argues that the police power is legitimately invoked solely "to protect individual liberty and private property against all manifestations of force and fraud." No other intrusion by the state is justified (Richard Epstein, *Takings: Private Property and the Power of Eminent Domain* [Cambridge, Mass.: Harvard University Press, 1985], p. 112; cf. his "A Theory of Strict Liability and Tort," *Journal of Legal Studies*, vol. 2 [1973]). Epstein concludes from his extreme Lockean assumption that "[all] regulations, all taxes, and all modifications of liability rules are takings of private property prima facie compensable by the state" (*Takings*, p. 95).

18. Joel Feinberg uses the phrase in his essay "Crime, Clutchability, and Individuated Treatment," in *Doing and Deserving: Essays in the Theory of Responsibility* (Princeton: Princeton University Press, 1970). Feinberg speaks of the criminal trial as a preliminary hearing "to establish whether the state has the right to get a defendant in its clutches" (p. 265). My use of the term differs: the state may take suspects into its clutches prior to trial and on the basis of reasonable suspicion.

can be as relatively harmless as being issued a parking ticket. But it reflects a potentially awesome power—think of the metal claws some municipalities lock onto our automobile tires if we don't pay our parking fine. The image of clutching makes present to us the problematic character of this phase of legal punishment: who are you, to take hold of me?

3.2.1 Pre-trial Detention   Clutching is connected to punishment in two ways. Almost everyone who is legally punished was at one point clutched—clutching is a precondition of legal punishment. But there is also a sense in which the act of clutching in itself constitutes punishment: for example, we often count time spent in pre-trial detention toward the serving of a convicted suspect's term of sentence. We might disagree over this latter point, that clutching itself constitutes punishment. Hobbes argues that what we call pre-trial detention is by definition not punishment, "because no man is supposed to be Punisht, before he be Judicially heard, and declared guilty."[19] But saying it isn't punishment doesn't mean it's not. The constitutional status of pre-trial detention— whether it counts as punishment—is contested. "Due process requires that a pretrial detainee not be punished."[20] In deciding whether pre-trial detention counts as punishment, "a court must decide whether the disability is imposed for the purpose of punishment or whether it is but an incident of some other legitimate governmental purpose."[21] In *Schall v. Martin* a majority of the Supreme Court ruled that the conditions of confinement of pre-trial detention (in this case, of juveniles) reflect the "regulatory" purpose of the state, where regulation is distinguished from punishment.[22] But Justice Marshall dissented:

> [The majority's] characterization of preventive detention
> as merely a transfer of custody from a parent or guardian

19. Thomas Hobbes, *Leviathan*, ed. Michael Oakeshott (New York: Collier Books, 1962), ch. 28, p. 233.
20. *Bell v. Wolfish*, 441 U.S. 520 (1978) at 535, note 16.
21. Ibid., at 538.
22. *Schall v. Martin*, 467 U.S. 253 (1984), pp. 269–70.

to the State is difficult to take seriously. Surely there is a qualitative difference between imprisonment and the condition of being subject to the supervision and control of an adult who has one's best interests at heart.[23]

Marshall also noted that the pre-trial detainee "suffers stigmatization and severe limitation of his freedom of movement."[24]

Marshall's suggestion that pre-trial detention is really punishment is part of a retributive criticism of this practice. In this view, we punish someone justly only when he is guilty of committing a wrong, and pre-trial detention violates this principle. Ronald Dworkin, for example, notes that the principle that a man is innocent until proven guilty accounts for "why it seems wrong to imprison a man awaiting trial on the basis of a prediction that he might commit further crimes if released on bail."[25]

It's important to distinguish retributivist objections to the very idea of pre-trial detention from retributivist objections to pre-trial detention that is punitive. Any retributivist at all aware that the ideals of justice must be realized by some process would have to acknowledge the necessity of detaining, at some point prior to a formal adjudication of guilt, a person suspected of committing a crime.[26] Andrew von Hirsch and his colleagues argue that

> [a] distinction should be observed between the system of sanctions (whose severity should be based on desert) and the sanctions necessary to maintain that system (which have to deter sufficiently to keep the system operating).

> Suppose one takes the position that there should be no pretrial detention, because a person does not deserve to be deprived of his liberty unless found guilty of an of-

23. Ibid., pp. 289–90.
24. Ibid., p. 291.
25. Ronald Dworkin, *Taking Rights Seriously* (London: Duckworth, 1978), p. 13.
26. The Supreme Court recognizes that the government may do this: see *Gerstein v. Pugh*, 420 U.S. 103 (1975), at 111–14.

fense. To preserve such a rule, however, it may still be necessary to make at least one exception—for absconders who might otherwise simply absent themselves from trial for any misdeed with which they had been charged.[27]

The Supreme Court argues, along the same lines as von Hirsch, that clutching, though it may violate retributive or desert-based principles, is justified as a "legitimate state objective . . . of protecting . . . society from the hazards of pretrial crime."[28] The retributivist might object to detention that is based on a prediction of a future violation of the law; on the other hand, the retributivist might recognize that to attain the justice she values requires certain institutions, and that to maintain these institutions, retributive ideals may have to be sacrificed to some extent. If we are to punish those deserving of society's condemnation, we must clutch, and we can clutch only suspects, not convicted criminals; that is simply a fact about our institutions. The retributivist who acknowledges the institutional requirements for attaining the retributive ideal might even recognize that as citizens we each have an *obligation* to let ourselves be clutched if we engage in an activity that might be presumed by a reasonable person to violate the criminal law. We might regard this duty as being just so long as we recognize as legitimate the state's authority to punish. Some of us *won't* recognize that authority, especially when clutching is carried out in an arbitrary manner—a distinct possibility, given the discretion accorded to the police and prosecutor.[29] Some will see clutching as coercion because they challenge the state's role as *parens patriae* or protector of our interests. In other words, when our particular concern is with

27. Andrew von Hirsch, *Doing Justice: The Choice of Punishments,* Report of the Committee for the Study of Incarceration (Westford, Mass.: Northeastern University Press, 1986), pp. 130–31, note. Von Hirsch was executive director of the Committee for the Study of Incarceration and principal author of this report.

28. *Schall v. Martin,* 467 U.S. 253 (1984), at 274. This case is specifically about pre-trial detention of juveniles, and the second ellipsis replaces the original phrase "the juvenile and."

29. Hart, "The Aims of the Criminal Law," p. 429.

the question "Who are *you* to punish?" our answer, as when we considered questions associated with lawmaking, will turn, not necessarily on utilitarian or retributive principles, but on our theory of legitimate state authority.

3.2.2 Political Crime   To justify the practice of clutching is to justify the authority of the state that clutches. In France in the 1830s the Fourierists challenged that authority. Some Fourierists claimed that "crime constitutes a political instrument that could prove as precious for the liberation of our society as it has been for the emancipation of the Negroes."[30] To these Fourierists some crimes, rather than being wrongs, were actions taken in the name of right and justice. Recently, in our own country, Raymond Luc Levasseur, a defendant accused of sedition under the Conspiracy Act of 1861, called himself a revolutionary who has vowed armed resistance to racism, South African apartheid, and "capitalist-backed wars," and he asked his jury: "Who are the real criminals? Those who oppose racist acts in South Africa or those who support government interests in South Africa?"[31]

Some people do not accept the state as "we"; to them, punishment is coercion of "us" by "them." These people question the justice of state punishment and the wrongness of crime. Is it just to punish those who are politically and socially excluded from, or oppressed and exploited by, the society whose values the criminal law upholds?

To some in a society, right, declared by the laws of the state and enforced by its police, does not seem right; and committing what the state regards as a wrong does not seem wrong. To the Fourierists, to Levasseur, to the blacks in Miami rioting because "They get everything, Nothing for us,"[32] what the state calls a crime may be an ultimately just and liberating act. To

30. *La Phalange*, January 10, 1837; cited by Michel Foucault in *Discipline and Punish: The Birth of the Prison*, trans. Alan Sheridan (1975; New York: Vintage, 1979), p. 289.
31. *New York Times*, January 12, 1989.
32. *New York Times*, January 18, 1989. See also my discussion in chapter 1, section 1.

these people, state punishment is not the vindication of right but a political means of repression masked as legal retribution.

We might distinguish from ordinary criminals the excluded, marginal, rebellious, and revolutionary who commit crimes in a society they regard as unjust, by calling them political criminals, and the actions they commit, political crimes. We are then faced with the question of the legitimacy of punishing political criminals.

The concept of political crime is an elusive one that has received some, but not enough, attention. Stephen Schafer distinguishes "ordinary" from "political" crimes but thinks that really the two blur.[33] Schafer suggests that every crime can be viewed as a challenge to the political system:

> All social systems design one or another kind of social order, and all construct norms and rules to ensure the effective operation of the particular society. The violation of any of these norms and rules, to one degree or another, endangers the smooth operation of the particular political order.[34]
>
> Shoplifting and robbery, for example, are criminal attacks against the value attached to private property, and even abortion and homosexuality are assaults only against single issues of the political power's ideology.[35]

Of course, not all criminals intend by their act to attack a particular "political power's ideology." Schafer distinguishes genuine from "pseudo" political criminals. The genuine political criminal is "inadequately socialized" and

> is ready to violate [the] dominating morality, even at the price of suffering the sanction, without being capable of developing regret, remorse, or the feeling of guilt, and

33. Stephen Schafer, *The Political Criminal: The Problem of Morality and Crime* (New York: Free Press, 1974), p. 27.
34. Ibid., p. 28.
35. Ibid., p. 29.

with the capability of being convinced that his immoral conduct is moral.[36]

Borrowing Gustav Radbruch's term *Überzeugungsverbrecher,* which Schafer translates as "the convictional criminal," he writes:

> The political criminal is "convinced" about the truth and justification of his own beliefs. . . . This element of "conviction" may serve as a distinguishing factor in discriminating the political criminal from the ordinary offender.[37]

The common criminal "almost always acts to fulfill his ego or personal interests,"[38] whereas the convictional criminal has an "altruistic-communal vision."[39]

Another theorist of political crime also distinguishes "conventional" from "political" crimes. In Austin Turk's view, the conventional criminal regards his polity's authority as essentially legitimate. But political criminals believe "that their life chances are excessively threatened or reduced by the actions (or inactions) of the authorities."

> [T]hey may challenge the authorities . . . by spontaneous or calculated, organized or unorganized dissent, evasion, disobedience, or violence. Such direct challenges to authority will at some point—depending upon the seriousness of the challenge as perceived and interpreted by the authorities—become intolerable enough to them to be either openly or "operationally" defined as political *crimes.*[40]

Turk cites as examples of political crimes the United Auto Workers' sit-down strike of 1936–1937 (charges included kid-

36. Ibid., p. 113.
37. Ibid., pp. 145–46.
38. Ibid.
39. Ibid., p. 148; cf. p. 112.
40. Austin Turk, *Political Criminality: The Defiance and Defense of Authority,* vol. 136, Sage Library of Social Research (Beverly Hills: Sage, 1982), p. 34.

napping General Motors plant guards, malicious destruction of property while rioting, criminal syndicalism, inciting to riot, and violating injunctions against picketing); violations of the 1723 Black Act (which mandated the death penalty for "blacking" one's face as a disguise in order to raid the gentry's property); and violations of the black codes passed in several Southern states in 1865–1867 and of the Jim Crow laws of the 1880s, which mandated segregation.[41]

With political crime the concern is not that of our philosopher. Those who view punishment as political coercion are bothered by the hurt punishment brings; but insofar as they are making an argument against punishing political crimes they oppose this hurt, not because they hold to the principle that it is never right to harm another, but because they believe that in some cases the hurt inflicted on the criminal *by the state* is unjust. Our philosopher is committed to opposing the spanking of children, but those opposed to punishment of political crimes are not necessarily so committed.

The problem of political crime—whether it is just to punish someone who acts in protest against the state—does not often arise within the practice of legal punishment. Occasionally it does. In September 1933, a large number of unemployed people marched to the Red Cross commissary in the city of Anacortes, Washington, and demanded a greater allowance of flour. Having been refused, the crowd left and entered the Skaggs grocery store, where many helped themselves to groceries without paying for them. Some were arrested and con-

41. Ibid., pp. 43–48. Turk cites favorably the work of another theorist of political criminals who gives as specific examples Stokely Carmichael, Daniel Ellsberg, Mark Rudd, and Ulrike Meinhof and Andreas Baader: Richard Moran, "Political Crime," Ph.D. dissertation, University of Pennsylvania, 1974, pp. 139–40, in Turk, *Political Criminality*, pp. 92–93. Also on the concept of political crime, see David Jones, *Crime, Protest, Community and Police in 19th Century Britain* (London: Routledge and Kegan Paul, 1982); and the works mentioned in a footnote listing those who have attempted to circumscribe what political crime means, in Schafer, *The Political Criminal*, pp. 10–11, note 5.

victed of rioting. The conviction was appealed, and the case was eventually heard by the Supreme Court of Washington. The appellants offered to prove the conditions of poverty and want among the unemployed of Anacortes and Skagit county, in order to show a motive and justification for the raid. One appellant argued:

> The groceries were taken, of course, but remember this; there is a higher law that says that a person holds his responsibility to himself first. There is a law of self-pres-ervation, and how can you expect a man to go against the most fundamental urges—the most prominent is the quest for food. Even the cave man in days gone by must have food.[42]

In another case, the defendants were convicted of depredation of government property when they threw or poured blood and ashes on the walls and ceilings of the Pentagon in a demon-stration against the design and possession of nuclear weapons. The defendants justified their actions as a "necessary defense to illegal possession by the U.S. of nuclear weapons," but were unsuccessful. The Court of Appeals affirmed the conviction.[43] In both cases judges were asked to consider the justice of punishment for actions committed in the name of a "higher" law. In both cases state punishment was deemed just.

In practice, when the question of political crime arises the issue gets transformed from what it is originally—a question of the legitimacy of state punishment—to the question of whether the defendant's action was "justified." In criminal-law doctrine, justification is distinguished from excuse. The difference is the same as that between being forgivably wrong (excuse) and being right (justified). When a person has acted

---

42. *State v. Moe*, 24 Pac. 2d 638 (1933). The court ruled that "eco-nomic necessity has never been accepted as a defense to a criminal charge. . . . In larceny cases [it] is frequently invoked in mitigation of punishment, but has never been recognized as a defense."

43. *U.S. v. Cassidy*, 616 F. 2d 101 (1979).

with justification he has no need of forgiveness.[44] If someone can show he committed an otherwise criminal act out of "necessity," his act is "justified" and is not considered a wrong:

> In a plea of necessity, the defendant admits performing the act charged and admits the act technically violated a law. The defendant contends that the conduct was justified because it was the only feasible way to avoid a greater evil and that it would be unjust to apply the law in the particular case.[45]

In the case involving defacement of the Pentagon, the Court of Appeals based its decision on whether the defendants' defense met the standards for the justification defense of necessity:

> Even if possession of nuclear weapons is illegal as defendants contend . . . the necessity defense is inapplicable. As sought to be applied here, essential elements of the defense are that defendants must have reasonably believed that their action was necessary to avoid an imminent threatened harm, that there are no other adequate means except those which were employed to avoid the threatened harm, and that a direct causal relationship may be reasonably anticipated between the action taken and the avoidance of the harm.[46]

44. Edward Arnolds and Norman Garland, "The Defense of Necessity in Criminal Law: The Right to Choose the Lesser Evil," *Journal of Criminal Law and Criminology*, vol. 65, no. 3 (1974), pp. 289–90.

45. Ibid., p. 294. An example of a successful necessity defense is *U.S. v. Ashton*, 24 F. Cas. 873 (C.C.D. Mass. 1834): sailors charged with mutiny justified their refusal to obey the captain's orders on the grounds that the ship was not seaworthy. The court held that if the ship was unseaworthy the conduct was not criminal. *State v. Moe* is an example of a failed necessity defense. Another is *Ex parte Milligan*, 72 U.S. (4 Wall.) 2 (1866): time of war doesn't justify trying a civilian before a military tribunal, because he could be tried in accordance with law at a later time. Cf. Arnolds and Garland, "The Defense of Necessity," p. 292.

46. *U.S. v. Cassidy*, 616 F. 2d 101, 102. See also *U.S. v. Simpson*, 460 F. 2d 515 (1972). Simpson entered the Local Board of the Selective Service System in San Jose, California, in 1970, opened a file

By having its judges apply standards within the practice concerning justification, the legal system avoids messy political issues.[47]

The question of political crime, then, seems to be a topic, not for legal practitioners, but for theorists who stand outside the practice. But although political crime has not been an especially urgent issue within the practice, some theorists have suggested that we treat political criminals differently from others. For example, Gustav Radbruch suggests that "criminals by conviction" (*Überzeugungsverbrecher*) are not "real" criminals and should be punished less harshly than is usual.[48] In the jurisprudential literature in our own country, the problem of political crime is occasionally brought up in the generalized form: can there be just deserts in an unjust society? For example, in a recent study of the justice of incarceration Andrew von Hirsch and his colleagues ask:

> Suppose that the laws serve chiefly the interests of a ruling class at the expense of others . . . in what sense, then,

---

drawer, doused the contents with gasoline, and set the files ablaze. He was arrested, indicted, and convicted of destroying government property and interfering with the Selective Service System. Simpson sought to introduce evidence that his actions were done to avert greater evil in the war zone in Vietnam. The trial judge and the Court of Appeals rejected this argument. The higher court ruled that an essential element of the defense is a reasonable anticipation of a direct causal relationship between the otherwise criminal act and the avoidance of harm. In this case, the court ruled, the war would obviously continue without regard to Simpson's action (Arnolds and Garland, "The Defense of Necessity," pp. 299–300).

47. Assuming that the judge permits the defense of necessity, which is often not the case. In *U.S. v. Berrigan*, 283 F. Supp. 336 (1968), at 339, the judge declared that the defense is outmoded in modern society. Also on the defense of necessity in the criminal law, see Comment, "Necessity Defined: A New Role in the Criminal Defense System," *U.C.L.A. Law Review*, vol. 29 (1981); and Rollin M. Perkins, "Impelled Perpetration Restated," *Hastings Law Journal*, vol. 33 (November 1981).

48. Gustav Radbruch, "Die Überzeugungsverbrecher," in *Zeitschrift für die gesamte Strafrechtswissenschaft*, vol. 44 (Berlin: Walter de Grunter, 1924), pp. 34–38.

are violations of [these] law[s] moral wrongs that deserve
to be condemned through punishment?[49]

They note that some theorists suggest that those who live on
the margin of society and violate its laws have reduced culpa-
bility. H. L. A. Hart, for example, writes that in general a violator may be deemed less culpable if at the time of the offense
he found himself, through no fault of his own, in a situation
where "conformity . . . was a matter of special difficulty for
him as compared with . . . persons normally placed." However, von Hirsch and his colleagues conclude that it is not the
role of the judge to decide "whether the defendant was sufficiently 'deprived' to deserve less punishment," for the judge's
"judgment would tend to be strongly colored by his own social
outlook. Perhaps it is asking too much of judges to resolve
these questions dispassionately."[50]

Another way to take into account the special nature of political crimes would be to reinvoke the principle of jury nullification. Typically juries are bound by the instruction of
judges; they are told the relevant law and asked to apply it to
what they determine to be the facts of the case. As Arnolds
and Garland explain, "[T]he doctrine of jury nullification
holds that jurors have the right to set aside the instructions of
the judge," in other words, to decide both the law and facts
on the basis of conscience.[51] In *Sparf and Hanson v. U.S.* this
principle was discredited:

> Public and private safety alike would be in peril, if the
> principle be established that juries in criminal cases may,
> of right, disregard the law as expounded to them by the
> court and become a law unto themselves.[52]

49. Von Hirsch, *Doing Justice*, p. 144.
50. Ibid., p. 146. The quotation from Hart is taken from ibid., pp. 145–46.
51. Arnolds and Garland, "The Defense of Necessity," p. 297.
52. *Sparf and Hanson v. U.S.*, 35 156 U.S. 51 (1895), at 101–2, cited in Arnolds and Garland, "The Defense of Necessity," p. 297.

Present practice leaves no room for informing the jurors of their power to bring in a verdict on the basis not of the law but of their own conception of right.[53] But the issue remains, and one practical formulation of the problem of political crime is whether we should allow jury nullification.

Thinking about political crime takes us to the very core of traditional concerns of political theorists, especially those of the seventeenth and eighteenth centuries—questions of obligation and legitimacy: Who is obligated to obey the state, and to what extent? Under what conditions can we speak of the laws of the state as right, and disobedience as wrong? These questions we think about mainly when we are concerned with the justification of the practice as a whole, when we are outside the practice deciding whether to assume a position within. But these questions are occasionally also of importance to the practitioner. That a coherent argument can be made against the punishment of those who commit political crimes (which is not to say that the argument is of much practical significance) suggests the importance of the retributive account of legal punishment. The retributivist sees the point of punishment as the meting out of just deserts, as the expression of society's condemnation of acts that violate a shared sense of right. The force of the argument against punishing political criminals derives from this retributive understanding of what punishment means: to punish the political criminal, the person on the margin who is excluded by society, who does not regard its laws as her laws, who had no say in and isn't served by those laws, is not really to punish but to oppress, to engage in some other practice. It is hard to see how the utilitarian could feel the force of this argument. The utilitarian might be outraged by punishment of a person accused of diminishing social utility who had in fact augmented social utility. But such a characterization of, for example, the outrage among the blacks in Miami in reaction to the actions of a largely white and Hispanic police force would be a feeble caricature.

53. Cf. Arnolds and Garland, "The Defense of Necessity," p. 297.

In practice there would be many difficulties in excluding punishment of political criminals: How would we decide that a looter violated laws protecting property as a protest against a society he regards as unjust, and not out of personal greed?[54] How would we make an objective determination regarding whether a person is excluded from a society, so that its laws aren't her laws? What would be the consequences for the legal system of allowing the defense of necessity, or of jury nullification? But that a coherent argument can be made at all against punishing political criminals suggests how indispensable the retributive account of legal punishment is.

3.3 Determination of Guilt

The person who is suspected of violating a law and is clutched may then, at the discretion of the prosecutor, be brought to trial for a determination of guilt. Some of the most difficult issues faced by prosecutors, defense attorneys, and judges are raised at this stage of the practice. For some of these issues, our position will depend on whether we are retributivists or utilitarians; for others, both retributivists and utilitarians are ambivalent.

3.3.1 Plea-Bargaining   Plea-bargaining refers to the exchange, between prosecutor and defendant, of reductions in charge for a plea of guilty. It is a sort of bargaining in the shadow of the law—though the idea of bargaining is a bit misleading, since there are going rates of exchange.[55] The reason often given for why the prosecutor would offer a plea bargain and why the judge would accept (which in practice is typically the case) is that this is a quick and easy way to avoid the costs

54. As was suggested in some newspaper accounts of looting that took place during the 1989 Miami riots (*Miami Herald*, January 18, 19, 1989).

55. Malcolm Feeley, *The Process Is the Punishment: Handling Cases in a Lower Criminal Court* (New York: Russell Sage Foundation, 1979).

of trials and cope with heavy caseloads.[56] Some scholars note, however, that plea bargains are not simply the result of a "threat of trial" by the defendant and a "threat of conviction" by the prosecutor, since often the defense couldn't afford a trial, and for some judges trials are so rare that they wouldn't mind one.[57]

Plea-bargaining pervades the practice of legal punishment. By some accounts 90 to 98 percent of all cases are resolved without trial.[58] Plea-bargaining is systematic, and sometimes even structurally induced. The New York Special Drug Court resolves felony drug cases in as little as six days rather than the usual six months, by offering repeat offenders charged with certain felony drug violations (for example, street-dealing of cocaine or crack) a reduced prison sentence in exchange for a plea of guilty before the case is presented to a grand jury. The defendant is told that if he does not accept the offer of the lower sentence that day, he will not be offered so short a sentence again. Often the defense attorney has little time to consider possible weaknesses in the prosecution's case, and the defendant has little time to consider the consequences of pleading guilty.[59] Prior to the establishment of this policy, felony drug cases would require on average eight court appearances and about six months before defendants agreed to plead guilty. With the negotiated plea, cases are typically disposed of in less than two months.

56. See Herbert S. Miller, William F. McDonald, and James A. Cramer, *Plea Bargaining in the United States* (Washington, D.C.: National Institute of Law Enforcement and Criminal Justice, Law Enforcement Assistance Administration, U.S. Department of Justice, 1978), p. v.

57. Feeley, *The Process Is the Punishment*, pp. 186–87.

58. See *New York Times*, February 12, 1975, p. 1; Feeley, *The Process Is the Punishment*, p. 186; and Suzanne Buckle and Leonard Buckle, *Bargaining for Justice* (New York: Praeger Publishers, 1977), p. 3 (but cf. p. 4).

59. *New York Times*, February 6, 1988, p. 1.

That plea-bargaining allows tremendous savings in resources is a strong "utilitarian" argument in its favor.[60] By one estimate, if we took all cases to trial we would have to quadruple the number of court personnel.[61] But there are compelling retributivist objections to plea-bargaining. Retributive justice demands that we punish a criminal only because he has committed a crime; when a defendant cops a plea, however, he is punished for a lesser offense that he did not commit, an offense which in some jurisdictions needn't be based on what actually happened:

> The judgment entered on the plea in such situations may be based upon no objective state of facts. It is often a hypothetical crime, and the procedure—authorized by statute—is justified for the reason that it is in substitution for a charge of crime of a more serious nature.[62]

There have been cases of pleas to attempted manslaughter, a crime which is logically impossible.[63] The retributivist might claim, then, that punishing a person who cops a plea violates the retributive principle that we punish only for an offense, in order to vindicate right.[64] Punishment, the purpose of which is to express our condemnation of a wrong, loses its meaning when applied to a person who cops a plea, because it fails to take seriously the nature of that wrong.

60. I use the word "utilitarian" here with some reservation, for the reason I explained in chapter 3, section 1, introduction.

61. Comment, "Official Inducements to Plead Guilty: Suggested Morals for a Marketplace," *University of Chicago Law Review*, vol. 32 (1964), p. 167; cited in Buckle and Buckle, *Bargaining for Justice*, pp. 27–28.

62. *People v. Griffin*, 166 N.E. 2d 684 (N.Y. 1960), cited in Abraham Goldstein, *The Passive Judiciary* (Baton Rouge: Louisiana State University Press, 1981), p. 41.

63. Goldstein, *The Passive Judiciary*, pp. 42–43. Goldstein notes that not all courts allow pleas to hypothetical crimes. Arizona, for example, recognizes a "public interest in an accurate criminal record for the defendant."

64. Cf. J. D. Mabbott, "Punishment," in Stanley Grupp, ed., *Theories of Punishment* (Bloomington: Indiana University Press, 1971), p. 48.

Perhaps this seems a trivial objection: the person who cops a plea deserves some punishment (if we assume that he wasn't coerced into confessing guilt although he was in fact innocent) and receives some punishment—what does it matter precisely how his offense is categorized? But an argument can be made that it does matter:

> The distorting effect of inaccurate pleas is obvious. They make the world of crime and corrections a world of fictions. . . . Probation officers submit reports describing cases of rape or armed robbery to judges and correctional officials who are then obligated by principles of legality to treat the offenses as less than they plainly are. . . . The charge scale is both inflated and deflated by the tension between the real and the legal offense. The lesser offense is assumed to be masking a greater offense, inviting suspicions and inquiries to pierce the formal record.[65]

The retributivist's criticism of plea-bargaining cuts even deeper. It's not just that to punish someone who cops a plea is to punish someone for a crime she didn't commit, but that for the retributivist, punishment must be deserved, and so plea-bargaining misses the point of why we punish. Kenneth Kipnis offers the analogy of "grade-bargaining" to make this point. He has us imagine the following agreement: If I graded your paper carefully, it would probably receive a D. If you would waive your right to a careful reading, I'd give you a B. Each of us would be better off: I don't have to spend time reading your paper, and you get a better grade. Most students would accept this bargain. But, Kipnis argues, this would be wrong. "Bargains are out of place in contexts where persons are to receive what they deserve."[66]

65. Goldstein, *The Passive Judiciary*, pp. 44–45.
66. Kenneth Kipnis, "Criminal Justice and the Negotiated Plea," *Ethics*, vol. 86, no. 2 (January 1976), pp. 104–5. Kipnis's analogy is clever, but it is misleading in at least one respect. The professor *chose* to assign an essay, rather than an easily graded true-or-false exam; neither the state nor the prosecutor in particular similarly "chooses"

Some criticize plea-bargaining also as a violation of due process and of the spirit of the adversarial system. Due process demands that the defendant be presumed innocent and not be coerced into confessing guilt.[67] But there is a great likelihood that individuals faced with the risk of going to trial for a serious crime, especially if circumstances "look bad" for them, are psychologically coerced by the plea bargain into admitting to a lesser offense and accepting less severe, though certain, punishment.[68] One case of such coercion has been described repeatedly in studies of plea-bargaining:

> San Francisco defense attorney Benjamin M. Davis recently represented a man charged with kidnapping and forcible rape. The defendant was innocent, Davis says, and after investigating the case Davis was confident of an acquittal. The prosecutor, who seems to have shared the defense attorney's opinion on this point, offered to permit a guilty plea to simple battery. Conviction on this charge would not have led to a greater sentence than

---

among alternatives to having a criminal justice system. (Thanks to Steve Krasner for suggesting to me that Kipnis's analogy is misleading.)

67. Herbert Packer, *The Limits of the Criminal Sanction* (Stanford: Stanford University Press, 1968), pp. 166–67.

68. See Justice Brennan's dissent in *N. Carolina v. Alford*, 400 U.S. 25 (1970); and Conrad Brunk, "The Problem of Voluntariness and Coercion in the Negotiated Plea," *Law and Society Review*, vol. 13, no. 2 (Winter 1979). The retributivist R. A. Duff, in his *Trials and Punishments* (Cambridge: Cambridge University Press, 1986), criticizes plea-bargaining by appealing to his Kantian interpretation of the purpose of legal punishment. Duff argues that the essential purpose of punishment is to "promulgate and to justify to the citizen rules which she can and should see that she ought to obey" (p. 144). Plea-bargaining undermines this purpose: "[I]f we obtain a guilty plea by offering [a defendant] irrelevant and improper inducements or threats, which are meant to provide her with a purely prudential motive for pleading guilty, that plea loses its meaning and its value; and we no longer address or respect her as a rational agent. Such induced guilty pleas are no doubt useful . . . but they should have no place in a just and rational criminal process; for they are destructive of its proper ends and values" (p. 141).

thirty days' imprisonment, and there was every likelihood that the defendant would be granted probation. When Davis informed his client of this offer, he emphasized that conviction at trial seemed highly improbable. The defendant's reply was simple: "I can't take the chance."[69]

In this case and others like it, not only is due process violated by the coercion of a bargain that in effect denies the defendant his right to trial, but the result of the negotiated plea is to punish an innocent person, which violates the weak "negative retributive principle."[70]

Plea-bargaining seems inconsistent with the ideals the retributivist finds immanent in the practice of legal punishment. A fully committed retributivist might claim that punishment of someone who cops a plea is not really punishment and should not be a part of the practice. There is a problem with this position, though. One must wonder how the retributivist can claim to have identified the ideal immanent in the practice if that ideal contradicts such a pervasive feature of the actual practice. Rather than dismiss such a significant part of our actual practice because it violates the retributive ideal, we might wonder whether the retributivist has got that ideal right. Plea-bargaining is just one example of prosecutorial discretion, and most social scientists agree that discretion penetrates the criminal justice system through and through. In fact, the

69. Albert Alschuler, "The Prosecutor's Role in Plea Bargaining," *University of Chicago Law Review*, vol. 36 (Fall 1968), p. 61; cited in Kipnis, "Criminal Justice and the Negotiated Plea," p. 98.

70. It would be impossible to know how many such cases there are, since we can't know for certain whether the defendant really was innocent. To the accusation that due process is violated, one might respond that the defendant maintains his right to trial even with plea-bargaining, and that the reason he avoids trial is not because the bargain coerced him but because he is uncertain about the outcome of the trial process, of its ability to determine the truth, and it is this uncertainty that is the coercive element. I find this response unconvincing. The uncertainty over whether the trial will determine the truth of his innocence creates unease and anxiety, but is not coercive.

argument is made, discretion is an *essential* feature of the practice:

> If our view of the courts is correct, efforts to banish bargaining from the courtroom will be futile; their most likely result will be to drive bargaining into more latent forms than it now takes and to make the protection of a clandestine system a powerful interest of all participants. In such a circumstance, the prospects for reforming bargaining will be much worse than they now are.[71]

The uncompromising retributivist sticks to her ideal in the face of facts about the actual practice that contradict that ideal. For her, such facts don't deny the ideal, but, rather, indicate how strong the need is for practitioners to become theoretically informed and for the actual practice to be reformed thoroughly by abolishing plea-bargaining. I do not find that position persuasive. As an immanent critic, the retributivist is committed to deriving her ideals from existing practice, and in the face of facts that point to how discretion is a pervasive, even an essential, feature of that practice, the retributivist who is unwilling to accommodate those facts and readjust her ideals is no longer an immanent critic. Immanent criticism requires adjusting ideals in light of the facts. But the retributivist need not give up the ideal that punishment expresses society's condemnation for acts it regards as wrong and that it vindicates right, even in the face of facts suggesting that this ideal is violated in the actual practice. There is a moderate retributive position that acknowledges the necessity of some discretion in the criminal justice system if that system is to maintain itself so that the retributive ideal can be attained at all. This moderate retributivism adjusts the account of the ideal practice to take into account the facts: there *is* a great deal of discretion in the system, and plea-bargaining is a pervasive, even essential, feature of the practice. Rather than oppose plea-bargaining in principle, the moderate retributivist un-

71. Buckle and Buckle, *Bargaining for Justice*, p. 164.

derstands plea-bargaining to be a necessary expedient for maintaining a system that lets us mete out just deserts at all; plea-bargaining is a sacrifice of justice for the sake of justice. The moderate retributivist can still be critical of plea-bargaining, by insisting that we negotiate pleas only when doing so is necessary for the maintenance of the practice through which we attain our ideals, and that when we negotiate pleas we do so in a way consistent with retributive ideals—for example, that we insist the plea offense be commensurate in moral gravity to the actual offense, so that even though a bargain is made, the demands of justice are satisfied. This retributivist does not give up her ideals, but she readjusts them to accommodate an implacable reality.[72]

3.3.2 Accountability   A standard answer to the question "Why punish this murderer?" is "Because she did it!" But our practice of legal punishment is not so cut and dried; assuming she did it, we want to know whether she intended to murder, and whether she could have helped doing so.

A central concept in our criminal law practice is that of *mens rea*, or "vicious will." In most cases we require *mens rea* to punish. There had to be a choice on the part of the offender to do a blameworthy act.[73] There are two categories of *mens rea*. One is a narrow sense that refers to the requirement of a mental state. Several statutes stipulate that *mens rea* in this narrow sense is required; its absence precludes criminal liability. For example, it's impossible to commit larceny without intent, since larceny is defined as theft with intent to deprive the owner of property. Manslaughter, too, by definition requires intent, or an awareness that one's actions cause substantial risk. The other sense of *mens rea* is a wider one

72. In the final chapter I shall say more about the moderate retributive position which I defend, which is in some respects consequentialist, but is nevertheless opposed to utilitarianism.

73. See the discussion in Sanford Kadish, *Blame and Punishment: Essays in the Criminal Law* (New York: Macmillan Publishing, 1987), pp. 65–67.

that refers to the requirement that in order for a person to be convicted she must be legally responsible. The law absolves those we do not expect to comply with the law, for example, infants and the insane.

The requirement of *mens rea* seems central to criminal law. The immanent critic, who is guided by the principle(s) immanent in the practice, either must account for this requirement by the principle(s) she derives from the practice or else must criticize the requirement as inconsistent with the purpose of the practice. Utilitarians have made both moves, neither of which seems convincing. Bentham uses his principle of utility to account for the wide sense of *mens rea*, the requirement of legal responsibility: since the primary purpose of punishing is to deter, it would be pointless to punish children and the insane, for they could not be deterred.[74] H. L. A. Hart has discredited Bentham's argument: "Plainly it is possible that the actual infliction of punishment on the insane or children may deter normal persons."[75] Richard Posner accounts for the narrow sense of *mens rea*, the requirement of a mental state: since the purpose of punishment is to promote economic efficiency, it would be counterproductive to punish those who don't intend to commit wrongs, for then we'd all have to spend resources to avoid the appearance of committing a wrong, which would be wasteful.[76]

Some utilitarians, rather than attempt to justify the *mens rea* requirement on utilitarian grounds, instead acknowledge that the requirement is inconsistent with utilitarianism and suggest that we should abolish it. Utilitarian proponents of a strict liability standard of accountability are in effect immanent critics, employing the principle they believe to underlie

74. Jeremy Bentham, *An Introduction to the Principles of Morals and Legislation* (1789; reprinted New York: Hafner Press, 1948), chapter 13.

75. H. L. A. Hart, "Prolegomenon to the Principles of Punishment," in Stanley Grupp, ed., *Theories of Punishment* (Bloomington: Indiana University Press, 1971), p. 369.

76. See my discussion of Posner, chapter 3, section 1.3.

the practice as a whole to criticize a feature of the actual practice that, in their view, is inconsistent with the ideals of the practice.[77] They argue that if the point of punishment is to prevent certain undesirable actions, intentions make no difference. Consider the case of an epileptic who in the midst of a seizure strikes a defenseless old man, severely injuring him. The utilitarian who insists on a standard of strict liability might insist on punishing the epileptic.[78] This would be to criticize our actual law, which allows for the defense (excuse)[79] of "involuntary action": we do not regard as culpable those who have no control over their bodily movements. Other utilitarians, and all retributivists, will be outraged by the idea of applying the strict liability standard to the epileptic; they will claim that this argument goes counter to the principles immanent in the practice. But the utilitarian and retributivist defenders of the "involuntary action" defense disagree about

77. Barbara Wootton, *Social Science and Social Pathology* (London: George Allen and Unwin, 1967); Barbara Wootton, "Diminished Responsibility: A Layman's View," in *Law Quarterly Review*, vol. 76 (1960), pp. 224–39.

78. As Richard Wasserstrom notes in his "Strict Liability and the Criminal Law," *Stanford Law Review*, vol. 12 (July 1960), pp. 731–45, strict liability statutes still involve some notion of fault. Wasserstrom describes an application of strict liability: in *State v. Lindberg*, 215 Pac. 41 (1923), a bank officer was convicted for borrowing excessive funds from his bank in violation of a statute prohibiting borrowing from his own bank. He believed the money had come from another bank. Wasserstrom imagines a different statute: "If a bank director borrows money in excess of a certain amount, from the bank of which he is director, then the director of any other bank shall be punishable by not more than ten years in the state prison." That imaginary statute would be unacceptable because it entirely does away with the concept of fault; the actual strict liability statute does not.

79. A defense doesn't deny the prima facie case "I didn't do it"; when I give a defense I acknowledge that "I did it" but claim I shouldn't be punished, because I have a defense. An excuse is a defense based on moral innocence. There are three types of excuses: involuntary action (I had no control over my body), deficient but unreasonable action (I had either a defect of knowledge or a defect of will, perhaps due to duress), and irresponsibility (perhaps I was insane) (Kadish, *Blame and Punishment*, pp. 82–87).

the principle justifying the defense. Both would defend the epileptic by saying that the epileptic couldn't help it. To the utilitarian, the moral force of this reason is that the epileptic couldn't have been deterred; to the retributivist, it is that the epileptic doesn't deserve our blame—she's not at fault. If we reflect on this example we will, I think, accept the retributive justification for the defense. The retributivist immanent critic, who believes that the point of punishment is to express condemnation and who can point to many features of the practice in justification of this claim, might respond that we can't properly call our treatment of those who lacked *mens rea* "punishment."

I believe the retributivist provides a more persuasive account of both the narrow and the wide sense of *mens rea*: we do not punish people who did not intend to do wrong or who were not legally responsible, because these people do not deserve our condemnation or righteous anger. Punishment is punitive, and these people do not deserve to be punished. Consider an insane serial killer who eats his victims and shows no sign whatsoever of remorse or of appreciating that it's wrong to kill or to engage in cannibalism. This person can't be kept in an ordinary prison cell because he will eat the hands off anyone who comes near. He is deranged and deadly.[80] We might want to lock him in an impenetrable cell on some far-off island, or perhaps execute him. But we would not do so as punishment (though it certainly would look like punishment). He can't be punished. He's not legally responsible; he can't help doing his evil deeds. It's inappropriate to judge him, just as it's inappropriate to judge a rabid dog who chews the limb off a young child.

3.3.3 Exclusionary Rule   In the previous section we considered defenses of moral innocence that excuse a person who physically did a wrong but claims to be undeserving of pun-

---

80. I refer to Dr. Hecter, a character in the recent film *Silence of the Lambs*.

ishment. In this section we shall consider another sort of defense, a defense based on a technicality. In this defense the offender claims, not that he was morally innocent and therefore undeserving of punishment, but that the authorities trying him violated a rule of procedure and therefore he should not be legally punished.

Some people who almost certainly have committed crimes are not punished, because the evidence that was used to convict them—either physical evidence, a confession, or an identification—was obtained illegally, in violation of the Fourth Amendment's proscription against unreasonable searches and seizures. The rule that excludes such evidence is not stated in the Constitution; it is a judicial construction that constrains prosecutors, juries, and trial court judges and is called the exclusionary rule. A glaring example of the cost of the exclusionary rule, but also of the reason for it, can be culled from the concurring and dissenting opinions of *Brewer v. Williams I*.[81] Williams had escaped from a mental hospital and was seen leaving a Des Moines, Iowa, YMCA with a bundle, presumably containing the body of Pamela Powers, for whose murder he was eventually tried. Two days later Williams turned himself in in Davenport, Iowa. His lawyer in Des Moines instructed Williams over the phone not to say a word while in the police car traveling from Davenport to Des Moines. Another lawyer in Davenport told the police not to question Williams about the abduction. This attorney was not permitted in the car. In the car, Detective Leaming gave what's called the Christian burial speech. He told Williams that it was going to snow and asked him to reveal where the body was so that Pamela's parents could give her a decent Christian burial. On the way to Des Moines, Williams led the police to the body. The Supreme Court ruled that what amounted to Williams's confession was wrongly admitted (in violation of the Sixth Amendment), and

81. *Brewer v. Williams I*, 430 U.S. 387 (1976). This was a Sixth Amendment case, not a Fourth Amendment case, but is still an example of how evidence that could incriminate is excluded, and what the costs of that exclusion might be.

Williams's conviction was reversed. In his concurring opinion Justice Marshall wrote:

> If Williams is to go free [which he doubts very much], it will be because detective Leaming, knowing full well that he risked reversal of Williams' conviction, intentionally denied Williams the right of every American under the sixth amendment to have the protective shield of a lawyer between himself and the awesome power of the State.[82]

In his dissent Chief Justice Burger replied:

> The Court errs gravely in mechanically applying the exclusionary rule without considering whether that draconian judicial doctrine should be invoked in these circumstances, or indeed whether any of its conceivable goals will be furthered by its application here.[83]

To some, the exclusionary rule, intended to uphold the rights of possibly innocent defendants by discouraging the police from overzealousness in their pursuit of criminals, obstructs the true purpose of legal punishment—the protection of society and control of crime. Others defend the rule by appealing to the importance of judicial integrity and the upholding of the rule of law and the rights of individuals, which the Fourth Amendment was constructed to protect.[84] The

82. Ibid., pp. 408–9.
83. Ibid., p. 420.
84. Of course, much of the debate over the exclusionary rule concerns the strictly constitutional issue of whether the rule is a constitutional command or a judicial construction. A famous debate about the theory underlying the exclusionary rule occurred between Yale Kamisar, who defends the rule on the grounds of both principle and consequences (as a check on police misbehavior, for example), and Malcolm Richard Wilkey, who opposes the rule because, in his view, it frustrates crime control (exchanges in *Judicature*, vol. 62, no. 2 [August 1978]; vol. 62, no. 5 [November 1978]; vol. 62, no. 7 [February 1979]). For empirical evidence to the effect that the exclusionary rule leads to the release of otherwise guilty persons, decreases public respect for the justice system, and is ineffective as a deterrent to police misconduct, see Steven R. Schlesinger, "The Exclusionary Rule: Have Proponents Proven That It Is a Deterrent to Police?"

problem of whether we should apply the exclusionary rule, like the problem of what we should criminalize, is not obviously resolved by either utilitarian or retributive principles. The exclusionary rule is defended by some retributivists who think we should go out of our way to avoid punishing innocent people, on the principle that we must punish only those who have committed a wrong: "It is far worse to convict an innocent man than to let a guilty man go free."[85] (On the other hand, the retributivist may wonder why we have an adversarial system of criminal justice that requires such measures as the exclusionary rule, as opposed to the inquisitorial system of many European nations.) But other retributivists oppose the exclusionary rule, on the grounds that we must punish the guilty and the exclusionary rule may prevent us from doing this. In deciding whether to use the exclusionary rule, we need to weigh not only competing values within the practice of legal punishment, but also other values, including some implicit in the Constitution. Application of the exclusionary rule means that sometimes a guilty person goes free. Yet refusal to apply it means that the courts have almost no power to enforce the Fourth Amendment. The value of the justice the retributivist

---

Judicature, vol. 62, no. 8 (March 1979). On the other side, Peter F. Nardulli, "The Societal Cost of the Exclusionary Rule: An Empirical Assessment," *Research Journal*, no. 3 (Summer 1983), pp. 585–610, argues that there is a low societal cost for the exclusionary rule. Nardulli claims that the success rate of motions to suppress physical evidence is only 0.69 percent, and in only 0.6 percent of all cases are convictions lost. See also Thomas Davies, "A Hard Look at What We Know About the Costs of the Exclusionary Rule: The NIJ Study and Other Studies of Lost Arrests," *Research Journal*, no. 3 (Summer 1983), pp. 611–92. Davies also concludes that there is a low societal cost to the exclusionary rule. Davies's article makes the excellent point that the exclusionary rule can have a significant effect on, without eliminating, police misbehavior, just as the 55 m.p.h. speed limit can have a beneficial effect without bringing about exact compliance. Instead of speeding at 80 under a 70 m.p.h. law, we now do 65 under a 55 m.p.h. law; our behavior is still illegal, but it is also safer.

85. *In re Winship*, 397 U.S. 358 (1969), at 372, Justice Harlan, concurring.

seeks must sometimes be weighed against other values that we, a people with many values and practices, cherish.

3.4 Sentencing

The suspect, having been clutched and tried as a defendant, then convicted, is a criminal who now must be sentenced, perhaps to become a convict. The next stage of legal punishment, sentencing, poses its own distinct issues. Again, not all of them can be resolved merely by a conception of the purpose of legal punishment, but some can.

Many of the controversies concerning sentencing hinge on the distinct but related questions: (1) should there be discretion (and, if so, how much); and (2) who should have it? Discretion in sentencing might mean individualized and often indeterminate sentencing, with discretion given to a parole board and not the judge. Discretion means, in this context, making exceptions in particular circumstances to general rules. In practice this means taking into account in determining her sentence the criminal's prior record, her prospects for rehabilitation, the danger posed to society, her family and economic situation, and other factors unique to the individual. It might also mean judicial discretion. In many jurisdictions judges are given wide latitude in setting a criminal's sentence. For example, in Connecticut the judge's sentencing options for the offense of armed robbery range from unsupervised release to twenty years' imprisonment. The judge's decision is not typically reviewable, nor need its justification be stated. This is troubling to many, especially in light of the wide variance in sentences judges deem appropriate. In one conference of federal trial judges, "a crime that drew a 3-year sentence from one judge drew a 20-year term and a $65,000 fine from another, though each judge was deciding on the identical set of facts."[86]

Some object to judicial discretion on the grounds that the legislature and not judges should decide issues that involve

86. Von Hirsch, *Doing Justice*, pp. 28–29.

moral judgments.[87] The prevalence of this view is reflected in the trend toward sentencing commissions, which are bodies authorized by the legislature to establish guidelines for judges to follow when sentencing. Sentencing guidelines establish a range of punishments that take into account the seriousness of the crime and the prior criminal record of the offender and also make allowances for aggravating and mitigating factors. Sentencing according to such guidelines is referred to as presumptive sentencing, since if the judge departs from the guidelines she must justify the departure. Discretion remains but shifts partly to the commission.[88]

On the first question—should there be any discretion in sentencing?—there is great disagreement, and divisions are often but misleadingly said to be along utilitarian-retributive lines. Some retributivists hold that there is a just amount of punishment that is deserved simply by virtue of the act committed by the criminal, so that there is no point taking into account other features of the individual in determining his sentence. Yet the demands of justice as fairness may require individualization of sentences. It would seem unjust, for example, to mete out the same fine to two criminals, one of whom was very rich, the other very poor, since the poor person would experience more punishment from the same fine. It's not clear, then, that retributivism commits us to oppose individualized sentencing. However, the retributivist does unambiguously oppose instances in which, though there are clearly acknowledged standards for what punishment is just, a judge departs from these standards for the sake of utility—when, for instance, he lets off with a sharp warning a prospective medical student so that she can pursue a career from which society would benefit, but sends to prison a person with no such bright future who committed the same crime.

87. Alan Dershowitz, "Who Decides and When?" in Hyman Gross and Andrew von Hirsch, eds., *Sentencing* (Oxford: Oxford University Press, 1981), pp. 343–48.
88. See Andrew von Hirsch, Kay Knapp, and Michael Tonry, eds., *The Sentencing Commission and Its Guidelines* (Boston: Northeastern University Press, 1987).

There are other issues concerning sentencing that can be resolved by choosing between utilitarian and retributive principles. Consider the question of whether we should give extended sentences to repeat offenders. Suppose that someone steals a car and that society normally attaches a five-year prison term to this crime. If this person has committed many previous crimes, a utilitarian might argue that he is dangerous and should receive an extended sentence. This would incapacitate him, keep him from harming society in the future. The retributivist immanent critic objects: justice demands a five-year sentence, not one day more or less. To keep the prisoner an extra day is to cause him to suffer for something he did not do, not really to punish him.[89] Extended sentences for repeat offenders are a part of our practice.[90] We use them, not, as in the case of plea-bargaining, as an expedient to help maintain the criminal justice system, but because we find it useful to incapacitate people we regard as dangerous.[91] For utilitarians, extending sentences of repeat offenders is entirely consistent with the purpose of legal punishment. For the retributivist, it is to engage in some other practice, not that of punishment.

This dispute between utilitarians and retributivists has some practical importance. Some recently established sentencing guidelines specify a rationale for sentencing. If the rationale for punishment is incapacitation of the offender, then factors such as predicted future behavior (based largely on prior criminal record) justify disparate sentences. If the rationale of punishment is desert, then such a disparity cannot be allowed. In

89. See Wojciech Sadurski, *Giving Desert Its Due* (Boston: D. Reidel, 1985), p. 255.

90. Cf. *Sas v. Maryland*, 334 F. 2d 506 (1964): "[I]t is within the power of the State to segregate from among its lawbreakers a class or category which is dangerous to the public safety and to confine this group for the purpose of treatment or for the purpose of protecting the public from further depredations."

91. It might be argued that a reason for extending sentences of repeat offenders is that they *deserve* more punishment. If this were true, the practice might be acceptable to retributivists.

other words, guidelines chart out a curve, with the *y*-axis length of prison term and the *x*-axis length of criminal record: a desert rationale implies a flat curve (longer criminal record does not merit longer sentence); an incapacitation rationale implies a steep curve (longer criminal record implies a more dangerous criminal and the need to incapacitate by extending the sentence). The Minnesota Sentencing Commission, for example, uses a combination of curves: a flat curve close to the origin reflects how the commission has chosen a desert-based rationale, but a steep curve further along the *x*-axis, that dictates harsher punishments for offenders with very lengthy criminal records, reflects the commission's desire to incapacitate those it regards as probable future threats to society.[92] That a chart with curves varying depending on one's theory of legal punishment is used in practice should excite the theorist of legal punishment. How rare it is for a theorist to have such a decisive practical impact! The privilege here given to the theorist, though, is itself a political decision, and the survival of sentencing commissions is by no means a certainty. The commissions have many politically powerful opponents, including judges who prefer to exercise discretion on their own.

The question of whether there should be discretion in sentencing or whether utilitarian considerations should weigh in the determination of particular sentences is distinct from the question of what punishment is, in general, commensurate with a given crime. Even if we think individual sentences determined at the discretion of the judge are legitimate, we still need to decide on what core level of punishment the individual sentence is based. Does commitment to either utilitarianism or retributivism help us with this question? Retributivists are often taken to answer this question by appealing to the *lex talionis*: punishment should fit the crime literally. But not only

92. See Andrew von Hirsch, "The Sentencing Commission's Functions," in von Hirsch, Knapp, and Tonry, *The Sentencing Commission and Its Guidelines*, pp. 3–15.

is this position not inherently retributive—we saw in chapter 3, section 1.1, that Bentham provides a utilitarian rationale for the *lex talionis*—most modern retributivists discredit it thoroughly. We shall see in the last section of this chapter that one retributivist, Hegel, argues, I think persuasively, that on this question of commensurability, retribution is of little help; ultimately the level of punishment society deems just for any given crime depends on the customs and conventions of that society, as well as on utilitarian considerations. One can hold that we punish for justice and insist that we only punish when doing so is consistent with justice, yet believe that the amount of punishment society regards as just is a matter of custom, convention, or utility, not something itself justified by the principle of retribution.

3.5 Infliction of Punishment

Probably most people outraged at the practice of legal punishment are disturbed by the actual infliction of pain. Certainly the hurt of punishment seems to many of us, including our philosopher, to demand justification:

> *Philosopher:* "So a man has committed a crime. It's done. Why hurt him? This won't undo the crime. If you hurt him, he'll only become more resentful, more antisocial, and so more likely to commit crimes. If you put him in prison this will still be true, but in addition he'll learn from his fellow inmates how to be a better criminal."[93]

By now we should see that to respond to our philosopher requires us to defend, not the whole practice of legal punishment, but the part of the practice that involves inflicting pain. Our philosopher may well be wrong about some of his asser-

93. Cf. Randall Barnett, "Restitution: A New Paradigm of Criminal Justice," *Ethics*, vol. 87, no. 4 (July 1977): "In prison [the criminal] learns the advanced state of the criminal arts and vows not to repeat the mistake that led to his capture. The convict emerges better trained and highly motivated to continue a criminal career" (p. 285).

tions.[94] But even if he were right, it would not follow that we should no longer inflict punishment. At best this philosopher gives an argument for punishing more effectively.

Distinguishing the issue of *how* (or whether) to inflict punishment from the issue of *how much* punishment we should inflict, and regarding the actual infliction of punishment as a subpractice distinct from sentencing, lets us focus on what is uniquely problematic about inflicting punishment. The problem here is not about how much pain we inflict, but that we inflict it at all instead of reacting in some other way upon the convicted criminal. One proposal, inspired by an antipathy to our present ways of inflicting punishment, has us respond to crimes, not by punishing, but by demanding restitution. Randall Barnett argues that the "paradigm of punishment is in crisis." Punishment is in crisis partly because of its uncertain moral status—we pity both victim and criminal—and partly because it is counterproductive, only encouraging more crime.[95] Barnett thinks we should change our present method of punishment by establishing a program of restitution wherein the offender compensates the victim.

Barnett goes further, saying we should *replace* punishment with restitution. He means to go beyond proposing a mere reform of the way we inflict punishment. Barnett's program includes a reconceptualization of crime and criminal justice:

> [Restitution] views crime as an offense by one individual against the rights of another. The victim has suffered a loss. Justice consists of the culpable offender making good the loss he has caused.[96]

94. Some studies suggest that punishment does deter. See Johannes Andenaes, "General Prevention—Illusion or Reality?" *Journal of Criminal Law*, vol. 43, no. 1 (July–August 1952), pp. 176–98; the same author's *Punishment and Deterrence* (Ann Arbor: University of Michigan Press, 1974); Laurence Ross, "Law, Science, and Accidents: The British Road Safety Act of 1967," *Journal of Legal Studies*, vol. 2 (1973), pp. 1–78; and Wilson, *Thinking About Crime*, ch. 7.
95. Barnett, "Restitution," pp. 281, 284–85.
96. Ibid., p. 287.

Instead of seeing in crime an offense against society, we now see an offense against an individual victim; Barnett compares this to a Kuhnian "shift of world-view."[97]

How simple! But how devastating to what matters to many of us. To Barnett, "the point is not that the offender deserves to suffer; it is rather that the offended party desires compensation."[98] Barnett achieves his paradigm shift by banishing from the criminal law all elements of desert and blameworthiness. But the retributivist believes that the point of this law *is* that the offender deserves to suffer.

Roger Pilon, responding to Barnett's article, makes just this point. He asks, "[I]f a rich man rapes a rich woman, are we really to suppose that monetary damages will restore the status quo, will satisfy *the claims of justice*?"[99] Pilon continues:

> The reduction of criminal wrongs to civil wrongs . . . bespeaks an all too primitive view of what in fact is at issue in the matter of crime. . . . Compensation does not reach the whole of what is involved—it does not reach the *mens rea* element. . . . The criminal has not simply harmed you. He has affronted your dignity.[100]

The argument underlying Pilon's point is that our criminal justice system is largely designed to express condemnation of certain blameworthy actions and that the criminal law in part articulates a social morality. In reducing criminal wrongs to civil wrongs, Barnett would change the practice of legal punishment beyond recognition.

Barnett's reduction of criminal to civil wrongs should remind us of some classical liberals' view that we cannot speak of injuries to the public or to state interest but only of injuries to individual interests recognized as rights. Barnett dismisses

97. Ibid.
98. Ibid., p. 289, quoting Walter Kaufmann, *Without Guilt and Justice* (New York: Peter H. Wyden, 1973), p. 55.
99. Roger Pilon, "Criminal Remedies: Restitution, Punishment, or Both?" *Ethics*, vol. 88, no. 4 (July 1978), p. 351, my emphasis.
100. Ibid., pp. 351–52 (cited in an order different from the original).

the idea of victimless crimes. First he objects to those defending the idea that there can be crimes that injure society
as a whole and not assignable individuals. Barnett writes: "It
might be objected that crimes disturb and offend not only
those who are directly their victim, but also the whole social
order." He then characterizes (in a rather unfair way) those
making this objection: "Restitution, it is argued, will not satisfy
the lust for revenge felt by the victim or the 'community's
sense of justice.' "[101] (But surely we can defend the idea of
victimless crimes without lusting for vengeance.) Barnett further defends his collapsing of crimes into torts while arguing
for decriminalization of activities most of us think are blameworthy:

> The effect of restitutional standards on the legality of such
> crimes as prostitution, gambling, high interest loans, por-
> nography, and drug use is intriguing. There has been no
> violation of individual rights, and consequently no dam-
> ages, and therefore, no liability. While some may see this
> as a drawback, I believe it is a striking advantage of the
> restitutional standard of justice. So-called victimless
> crimes would in principle cease to be crimes. As a con-
> sequence, criminal elements would be denied a lucrative
> monopoly, and the price of these services drastically re-
> duced. Without this enormous income, organized crime
> would be far less able to afford the "cost" of its nefarious
> activities than it is today.[102]

The practical implications of Barnett's suggestion are stag-
gering. It's not just that with Barnett's system we'd have no
remedy against someone who delights in torturing deer (for
deer possess no rights and therefore cannot demand restitution).[103] This might be upsetting enough, but I'd be even more

101. Barnett, "Restitution," p. 295.
102. Ibid., pp. 300–301.
103. Franklin G. Miller, "Restitution and Punishment: A Reply to
Barnett," *Ethics*, vol. 88, no. 4 (July 1978), p. 359. Of course, Miller
intends to be clever, and I do not mean to suggest that he fails to see
what I regard as the more serious objection. Miller points out also

bothered by the prospect of a free market in heroin and crack; or that if I had no surrogate (i.e., next of kin—but who would count?) someone could murder me without being taken off the streets or even reproached. My objection is not merely that, because those who use crack usually become violent, I'd be afraid to live in a society where it was legal to obtain crack. The restitutionist can point out that once the crack addict does become violent and injures me, I can seek restitution—this is a slight comfort. My objection is to living in a society where it is likely that using drugs such as crack will no longer be regarded as wrong.[104]

Pilon observes that in effect Barnett offers a paradigm not of criminal but of civil justice.[105] There are good reasons to think Barnett is offering us, not a reform of our practice of legal punishment, but a new practice.[106] But although Barnett insists on calling his theory of restitution a paradigmatic break with punishment, a careful reading of his proposal in the end belies his exaggerated claims. For the offender who fails to pay,[107] Barnett suggests "confinement to an employment project." And if the offender proved not to be "trustworthy," he would have to remain in the project, away from his family. Barnett also tells us that "if a worker refused to work, he would be unable to pay for his maintenance. . . . If he did not make restitution he could not be released."[108] Barnett refuses to call this punishment; perhaps he is too intent on advancing his

---

that Barnett leaves no room for dealing with such offenses against society as tax evasion, damage to public property, and obstruction of justice.

104. I advance this objection with some hesitation: if it's wrong to use crack, is it also wrong to use marijuana? alcohol? tobacco? Who decides?

105. Pilon, "Criminal Remedies," p. 350.

106. It's difficult to decide what counts as our practice, and what changes to it would count as constituting a new practice. We shall consider this difficult and crucial problem in the next chapter.

107. Presumably, if Barnett's ideas were implemented there would be no "criminals," only "offenders."

108. Barnett, "Restitution," p. 289.

ideas on restitution as a paradigmatic revolution to see the obvious point that any program of restitution, including his own, must rely on punishment as a threat. Barnett, searching vigorously for some remedy for crime that avoids the moral objectionability of our way of punishing, relies ultimately on another method of inflicting punishment; it's just that Barnett does not think we should call it punishment.[109]

Barnett is right to be troubled by our present method of inflicting punishment. Many questions plague us: Why inflict punishment if doing so only makes our crime problem worse? Why punish if between sentencing and punishment the criminal reforms and makes restitution?[110] Should we use exemplary punishments?[111] Should we use private prisons, because they are more cost-efficient? Should we execute criminals? By seeing the infliction of punishment as but one part of this broader practice, we can focus on the practical question of alternatives to our present methods of inflicting punishment.[112] Barnett cannot help us with these questions, because, according to his understanding of the purpose of criminal law, we don't need to punish crimes at all. I do not accept Barnett's interpretation of our practice. Although he agrees that our criminal justice system is intended to realize justice, his understanding of justice as nothing but restitution for violations

109. Barnett walks a fine line between offering radical and immanent criticism. In characterizing his proposal as a paradigmatic revolution, he reminds us of the radical critic, unwilling to accept the premises and principles underlying our practice of punishment. But Barnett fails to sever his ties with the practice completely.

110. Robert Nozick, in his *Philosophical Explanations*, says we should not (Cambridge, Mass.: Harvard University Press, 1981), p. 385.

111. Exemplary punishment is punishing a criminal particularly harshly as an example to others. Retributivists would say this is unjust; many utilitarians would say it is justified.

112. Many object to incarceration, but it is difficult to think of a satisfactory alternative. Examples of alternatives include warning and release; intermittent confinement that is not residential; and restitution in various forms, with back-up sanctions. See, for example, the discussion in von Hirsch, *Doing Justice*, pp. 119–22, 137–39.

of individual rights leaves him unable to account for why we *punish* for justice. We *do* punish, and not merely to compensate victims. Rather than adjust his ideal to account for what we actually do, Barnett sticks to the ideal and in effect offers us a new practice. But because it diverges so greatly from the ideals we do share, the practice he offers is not one I think we should want, or will be likely ever to have.

4. A Consequential Retributivism

The retributivism I have defended in this chapter is a modified retributivism. It acknowledges that the ideal of justice sometimes has to be adjusted in light of the facts, and in particular, of institutional requirements. There's no sense in holding to ideals if the institutions which let you realize your ideals are doomed to failure as a consequence. The retributivism I defend is not a compromise with utilitarianism, but it is in a sense consequentialist. I never hold that we should decide whether to punish by making a utilitarian calculation. Yet I am willing to say that if it is necessary to plea-bargain in order to maintain the system that lets us attain the retributive ideal at all, then we should plea-bargain.

The retributivism I defend is not always opposed to utilitarianism. The principle to which I hold demands that we punish in order to express society's condemnation of actions it regards as wrong, to mete out just deserts, and to vindicate right. On some issues, this principle is not specific enough to dictate what we should do. We saw in chapter 3 that utilitarians declare that we should punish only when doing so augments social utility. Bentham lists several cases "unmeet" for punishment, cases in which punishment should not be inflicted even though it is deserved. Retributivists who hold to what we called the positive retributive principle, which insists that we must punish those who are guilty of a crime, insist that we punish even though doing so is opposed to the principle of utility. Retributivists and utilitarians seem to clash head on regarding these cases, but they needn't. Some retributivists see a limit to what their retributive principle can determine. They acknowledge that their principle can't necessarily say how much punishment a criminal should receive, and in considering *that* question they are willing to take into account considerations normally thought to be "utilitarian." For example, Hegel writes:

> The various considerations which are relevant to punishment as a phenomenon and to the bearing it has on the particular consciousness, and which concern its effects (deterrent, reformative, etc.) on the imagination, are an essential topic for examination in their place, especially in connexion with modes of punishment, but all these considerations presuppose as their foundation the fact that punishment is inherently and actually just.[113]

Hegel insists that the reason we punish at all is to vindicate right and mete out justice, but in determining the *mode* of punishment Hegel is willing to take into account the future good a particular mode of punishment would bring about. Hegel recognizes there are limits to what the principle of retribution can determine: "[T]he qualitative and quantitative characteristics of crime and its annulment [punishment] fall . . . into the sphere of externality. In any case, no absolute determinacy is possible in this sphere."[114] Indeed, Hegel believes that the level of punishment appropriate for any given crime depends on the condition of the society that punishes: "A penal code [*Strafkodex*] . . . is primarily the child of its age and the state of civil society at the time."[115] In societies that are "internally weak," punishments must be harsher, in order to set an example, but in a society that is internally strong [*in sich fest*], punishment needn't be so severe.[116]

113. Hegel, *Philosophy of Right*, trans. T. M. Knox (London: Oxford University Press, 1952), par. 99, Remark.
   114. Ibid., par. 101, Remark; cf. par. 214; par. 218, Remark.
   115. Ibid., par. 218, Remark.
   116. Ibid., par. 218, Addition.

Justice may be indifferent to one sentence as opposed to another if, according to social norms, both suitably express our condemnation of the act. In choosing between two such sentences the retributivist can, without sacrificing the retributive ideal, appeal to considerations normally taken as utilitarian. This is what Hegel does. To look forward to the consequences of punishing in such cases is not to compromise retribution for the sake of utility; it is not to reduce retribution to a necessary but not sufficient condition for punishment and to let the utilitarian ultimately determine whether we should punish, as von Hirsch would have it.[117] Rather, it is to take the retributive ideal as far as it goes, and only when it can go no further, to invoke considerations normally taken as utilitarian.

I believe that retribution has been dismissed by many theorists of punishment either because it is conflated with revenge or because it is taken as a deontological theory, oblivious to consequences, and neither a position advocating vengeance nor one that holds to justice "though the world perish" is attractive. But the retributive position I defend is neither a revenge theory nor deontic; and I believe it offers the best account of why we do and therefore how we should punish.

117. Cf. my discussion in chapter 3, section 2.4.

5

Immanent Criticism of an Essentially Contested Practice

1. Introduction

In chapter 3 we examined two conflicting accounts of why we punish, of the justification of the practice; the utilitarian believes we punish to augment social utility, whereas the retributivist believes we punish to express society's condemnation of acts it regards as blameworthy, to vent its righteous anger, and to vindicate right—we punish for justice. We said that in choosing between the two principles we are deciding which ideal on the whole better accords with the purpose of the practice, and that ultimately to decide that question we must step inside the practice and see what is done. In chapter 4 we did just that. There I argued that central features of legal punishment are best accounted for by the retributivist ideal. In chapter 4 we also saw how other features of the actual practice diverge from the retributivist principle, that these features are inconsistent with the retributivist account of the purpose of the practice. The retributivist argues that punishing a person who cops a plea, or someone who is insane, or a person whose act of wrong was done in the name of some higher law or as a political act, or with an extended sentence because the criminal is a repeat offender, is not really "punishment." In suggesting this we were supposing that there is a practice called legal punishment that has a certain meaning and accords with a certain principle, and that an action that is nominally part of the practice is essentially or by right excluded from it if the action can't be accorded with that principle. We assumed that the features that accord with the retributivist ideal are somehow "central," a claim that itself demands justification. In other words, we assumed that there is a practice of legal punishment that is *essentially* retributive, and that the utilitarian is somehow *mistaken* about the meaning and purpose of punishment. In this chapter we shall consider what is wrong with this assumption and what its rejection means to those who would defend retributive (or, for that matter, utilitarian) immanent criticism.

The retributivist claims that certain features of the actual practice aren't really part of the practice, aren't really punishment. This leads to the question: How do we know what counts as a practice and determine what the practice includes, or which features are "central"?

2. What Counts as a Practice: The Turn to Interpretation

What might we mean when we call the spanking of a child or the arrest, conviction, and incarceration of a person a practice?[1] The *Oxford English Dictionary* tells us that the word "practice" can mean "a habitual doing or carrying on of something." But not everything we do habitually is a practice, and sometimes to do something out of habit is not to engage in it as a practice. I might say I have a bad habit of biting my nails, but I would be unlikely to say that I engage in the practice of nail-biting. It seems, then, that a practice is more than an action we do over and over again. The notion that a practice

---

1. In chapter 1 we considered John Rawls's account of a practice: a practice is defined by fixed rules. But we criticized this account, on the grounds that many practices don't have fixed rules.

is something "carried on" implies that it is intended; we don't call the earth's rotation about the sun a practice, even though it occurs repeatedly. A practice, rather, seems to be an action or set of related actions that is intended or has some purpose. It makes sense to ask of a practice, why do we do it?

When someone engages in a practice with which we are familiar, we can recognize this and guess at why that person acts so. Of course, we might be wrong: we might see an adult spank a child and guess that this was punishment, but they might just be playing some game. Some sort of principles or standards are involved in practices, so that when we observe a spanking, or an execution, we can suppose that certain things led up to this action and were the reason for it. We could go up to the adult and say, "Why are you punishing this child? Did she do something wrong?" And the adult might say either yes and explain what mischief the child had been up to, or no and perhaps explain the game they are playing that looks like but isn't punishment (we are assuming that this is some fictitious world where adults don't say "None of your damned business").

There is a funny thing about practices, though. They are the sorts of things we recognize as having a meaning or purpose, but often we can't easily say what that meaning or purpose is. Spanking a child and arresting, convicting, and incarcerating a person are practices in our society; but how do we know what meaning or purpose these practices have? What if we disagree?

The view I shall take is that we "know" the meaning or purpose of a practice by an act of interpretation.[2] It is a non-foundationalist view.[3] A foundationalist believes that practices

2. Several issues are raised by the claim that we "know" by interpretation: Knowledge in what sense of the word? Can interpretation ground practices (or, in the language of hermeneutics, can interpretation ground signs)? Why say we can only interpret the meaning of a practice—can't we understand a practice's meaning, i.e., truly know it? The line I shall take is that in the case of legal punishment the consensus is that we can't know; punishment is an essentially contested practice.

3. Here I borrow terms used by Don Herzog in *Without Founda-*

have fixed grounds which justify them; that we can prove an action is right by absolute principles about which we can have certain knowledge. According to the foundationalist, we can be mistaken about why we do what we do, about the meaning of our practices. A practicing Jew or Muslim who refuses to eat pork on the grounds that doing so would bring forth divine retribution, when in fact the taboo arose for ecological and economic reasons (see chapter 2, section 5), is, according to the foundationalist, *wrong* about why she does not eat pork. Nonfoundationalists take a different position. Practices, in their view, have no absolute grounds; the origin of a practice, its natural cause, needn't be connected with the purpose the practice has now.[4] The nonfoundationalist claims that ultimately a justification of a practice ends with the fact that this is what we do. In answering the question, Why do we do this? all we can do is construct reasons until eventually those who share in the practice are satisfied and stop asking "why" questions. If someone persists in asking, "But why is *that* a good reason?" eventually we can only shrug our shoulders. The nonfoundationalist believes there are no transcendent principles to which we can point that ultimately ground our practices and force an end to "why" questions. The nonfoundationalist does not deny that there can be justification; she claims, not that there is no sense in which we can say someone is right or wrong, that there are no grounds for justifying what we do; but, rather, that ultimately justification comes to an end, and that that end is a set of convictions and beliefs which *do* provide grounds, but which themselves cannot be further justified.[5]

---

tions: Justification in Political Theory (Ithaca: Cornell University Press, 1985), pp. 24, 225.

4. We saw that this was Nietzsche's position; see chapter 2, section 2.1.

5. A particularly intriguing version of nonfoundationalism is provided by the philosopher Ludwig Wittgenstein, a nonfoundationalist with respect not only to social practices but also to claims in the natural sciences and mathematics. In *On Certainty*, trans. Denis Paul and G. E. M. Anscombe (New York: Harper and Row, 1969), Witt-

Commitment to nonfoundationalism means that in thinking about the justification of legal punishment, no account in itself is privileged; what does privilege an account is its ability to persuade to a satisfactory degree those who view the practice differently.[6] As a nonfoundationalist, I can't resolve the debate between utilitarians and retributivists by appealing to some transcendental standard by which we can say that either utilitarianism or retributivism is *wrong*, but only by arguing that retributivism offers a better *interpretation* of what punishment is.

The view that interpretation is the way to come to the meaning of practices and even to a conception of what counts as and constitutes a practice is central to the recent work of Ronald Dworkin.[7] Dworkin argues that in interpreting a practice we begin with some pre-theoretical, intuitive notion of it. The act of interpretation itself begins when we imagine this act or set of actions we assume is a practice to be a set of rules with a value or purpose or principle that guides the rules and would warrant a change of actual practice should its practitioners begin to act counter to this purpose or principle. Dworkin argues that we give constructive interpretations of practices, interpretations that are concerned with the purpose not

---

genstein takes the position that "to be sure there is justification; but justification comes to an end" (par. 192). Our justifications ultimately rest on a shared system of convictions, what he calls the "inherited background," that itself cannot be justified (cf., for example, pars. 94, 102, 105, 141–44, 298). Wittgenstein writes: "We all believe that it isn't possible to get to the moon; but there might be people who believe that this is possible and that it sometimes happens. We say: these people do not know a lot that we know. And, let them be never so sure of their belief—they are wrong and we know it. If we compare our system of knowledge with theirs then theirs is evidently the poorer one by far" (par. 286). But all Wittgenstein says is that "we say" that "they are wrong," not that in fact "they are wrong." For Wittgenstein, justification rests on "persuasion" (pars. 262, 609–12, 669).

6. What counts as a satisfactory degree will depend on the particular context in which we disagree and are drawn to the activity of justifying.

7. Ronald Dworkin, *Law's Empire* (Cambridge, Mass.: Harvard University Press, 1986).

of the author but of the interpreter of the practice.[8] The practice is a "form of life" and has a vocabulary that is shared by
people, who may disagree about the purpose of the practice
while nevertheless sharing in it as a form of life.[9]

Dworkin emphasizes that what is at stake in our interpreting
practices is our ability to criticize and change the practice.
Our interpretation may lead us to change our view of what
the practice requires. Upon our interpretive effort we may find
that the practice makes unjust demands that turn out not really
to belong to the practice; they are condemned by principles
needed to justify other demands the practice imposes.[10] The
act of interpretation is in a sense constitutive of the practice
itself. In Dworkin's view there is a dialectic of sorts: how we
view the practice shapes what we think it requires; but, also,
how we view what is required may shape how we interpret
the practice. The implication of this view is that our practices
have no foundation other than the interpretations we give to
them.

We might think that this view that we know the meaning
or purpose of practices, and even what constitutes the practice, on the basis of interpretation is a rather subjectivist account: aren't practices out there, aren't their purposes waiting
to be discovered and understood? But if we hold a dialectical
account of interpretation, we can meet the charge of subjec-
tivism by noting that our interpretation *is* of a practice—all
that we say about the practice is about something of which
we have some pre-theoretical ideas whose source is "out
there." It is in this respect that the critical work our interpretation does is immanent criticism. In saying that we can
only *interpret* the meaning of the practice, we are owning up
only to the idea that we can have practices that don't obviously
serve any single purpose and may serve competing purposes,
and that we may disagree about what the purpose(s) is (are)
though we still all engage in them.[11] There is no single purpose

8. Ibid., p. 52.
9. Ibid., p. 63.
10. Cf. ibid., p. 204.
11. On the idea that some of our concepts are essentially con-

that everyone would (or anyone is compelled to) agree accounts for everything significant about the practice. Any claim about the purpose of such practices must be an interpretation. Our discussion of the practice of legal punishment in chapters 2–4 suggests that it is such a practice. To further illustrate this point, that legal punishment is a practice with conflicting principles immanent in it, I include an appendix that discusses how, in what appear to be two instantiations of the practice of legal punishment, aspects of the practice can be accounted for only by distinct and mutually exclusive interpretations of its purpose.

3. An Objection to the Retributive Interpretation of Punishment

I have defended the retributive interpretation that we punish for justice and have even advanced the argument that to punish people in a way that violates the retributive ideal is to engage in some practice other than punishment. But there is a problem with the claim that features of legal punishment that violate the retributive ideal aren't part of the practice: they *are*. It's unconvincing to say that punishing a person who cops a plea, or who is insane, or whose act of wrong was a political act of protest is not really punishment. To call any of these "punishment" would be good English. Slightly more convincing is the retributivist's argument that grammatically we can't punish someone who merely violates a regulation but does nothing blameworthy; we can only inflict upon this person a penalty.[12] But ordinary language is ambiguous even here: we

---

tested—that is, that we all use the concept (or engage in a practice) although we disagree about what the concept (or practice) is all about—see W. B. Gallie, "Essentially Contested Concepts," in Gallie, *Philosophy and the Historical Understanding* (London: Chatto and Windus, 1964).

12. See Joel Feinberg, "The Expressive Function of Punishment," in *Doing and Deserving: Essays in the Theory of Responsibility* (Princeton: Princeton University Press, 1970); and R. A. Duff, *Trials and Pun-*

speak of the murderer receiving the death "penalty." And the claim that it's impossible to punish someone for something she did not do is not at all nonsense, yet nevertheless there is precedent in ordinary language for saying the opposite. The ambiguities in the word "punishment" reflect the tensions in the practice of legal punishment.

The difficulty the retributivist immanent critic faces is that legal punishment is an essentially contested practice: both utility and retribution are principles immanent in the practice. Recent philosophical discussions about utilitarian and retributive theories of punishment have arrived at what might seem to be a similar conclusion: both principles are seen to be "there" in the practice, sharing in what might be called a division of justificatory labor; and neither the utilitarian nor the retributive theory alone is sufficient—we need some optimal mix. In the next section I shall consider the major compromise approaches and discuss why I think that although they are right to acknowledge that both principles are at work in legal punishment, in trying to reconcile the two they fail to take seriously enough how each principle lays claim to be the sole principle of the practice.

4. The Contemporary Utilitarian-Retributive Debate

Contemporary theorists of punishment have sought to reconcile utilitarianism and retributivism. Historically, they did this in the context of defending utilitarianism against the objection made by retributivists that the principle of utility, consistently applied, recommends in principle the punishment of the innocent, for surely in some cases doing this would be "optimific."[13] Most utilitarians saw this charge—violation of

---

ishments (Cambridge: Cambridge University Press, 1986), who argues that if it doesn't fulfill the Kantian requirement that the defendant "participate" in the punishment by understanding why she's being punished, then it's not "punishment" (p. 28; cf. pp. 37–38: the insane "can't" be punished).

the retributive demand to punish only the guilty—as a valid concern and sought to preserve their utilitarian account while recognizing the retributive demand.[14] By taking what has been called "the middle way,"[15] they understood the two principles as sharing in a division of justificatory labor. In one version, the retributivist is said to justify how we punish in particular cases by pointing to the rules of the practice, one of which is to punish only the guilty, whereas the utilitarian is said to justify why we have the practice to which the rules belong.[16] According to this rule-utilitarian account, the utilitarian avoids the unacceptable position of justifying punishment of the innocent, without violating the principle that we should do what has the best consequences, by claiming that *in the long run* it's best to follow (the best) rules.[17] In another version, the

13. See Igor Primoratz, *Justifying Legal Punishment* (Atlantic Highlands, N.J.: Humanities Press International, 1989), chs. 2–3; J. J. C. Smart, *An Outline of a System of Utilitarian Ethics* (Adelaide, Australia: Melbourne University Press, 1961); C. L. Ten, *Crime, Guilt, and Punishment* (Oxford: Oxford University Press, 1987). Some utilitarians deny that their principle justifies punishment of the innocent. To punish someone who has not been found guilty of a crime would not be really to punish them. See Anthony Quinton, "On Punishment," *Analysis*, vol. 15 (June 1954), p. 138; K. Baier, "Is Punishment Retributive?" *Analysis*, vol. 16 (1955), p. 27; C. K. Benn, "An Approach to the Problems of Punishment," *Philosophy*, vol. 33 (October 1958), p. 331. But see Arnold Kaufman, "Anthony Quinton on Punishment," *Analysis*, vol. 20, no. 1 (October 1959), p. 13; and K. G. Armstrong, "The Retributivist Hits Back," *Mind*, vol. 70 (October 1961).

14. One exception is J. J. C. Smart, who faithfully abides to his utilitarian tenets: if it would augment social utility, he demands, why not punish the innocent? "Extreme and Restricted Utilitarianism" in Michael Bayles, ed., *Contemporary Utilitarianism* (Gloucester, Mass.: Peter Smith, 1978), p. 113.

15. Primoratz, *Justifying Legal Punishment*, ch. 6.

16. John Rawls, "Two Concepts of Rules," in Bayles, ed., *Contemporary Utilitarianism*, pp. 59–98. See also R. M. Hare, *Moral Thinking: Its Levels, Method and Point* (Oxford: Oxford University Press, 1981), for another effort to incorporate retributivism, understood as rule-following, into a utilitarian theory.

17. I understand Rawls to put forth a different argument: to engage in the practice is to justify actions of the practice by appealing to its rules; we do this, not because these rules are best, but because

retributivist is said to justify whom (only the guilty) and how much (an amount commensurate to the evil) we may punish, whereas the utilitarian is said to justify why we punish at all (to augment social utility).[18] By seeing each principle as fulfilling a different function, these theorists claim to give a utilitarian justification of punishment that respects the retributive demand that we not punish the innocent.

These attempts at an attractive and neat reconciliation are widely accepted.[19] Their various proponents share a widespread prejudice among us that contradiction and conflict among principles are bad. But I believe that the reconciliation these theorists have achieved is illusory. There is no simple division of justificatory labor such that utility and retribution are compatible principles, both at work fulfilling different functions within the practice. Legal punishment is an essentially contested practice. To say, as does Rawls, that utilitarians justify why we have the rule-guided practice while retributivists justify actions of the practice by appealing to those rules is to give an inaccurate account of the arguments actually

---

we must appeal to them if we are to engage in the practice. Rawls says his point is "a logical point" and that "[t]here is no inference whatsoever to be drawn with respect to whether or not one should accept the practices of one's society" ("Two Concepts of Rules," p. 97).

18. H. L. A. Hart, "Prolegomenon to the Principles of Punishment," in Stanley Grupp, ed., *Theories of Punishment* (Bloomington: Indiana University Press, 1971). Unlike Rawls, Hart casts his theory as a compromise theory, in that he acknowledges that our practices have conflicting principles, and so we need a compromise (H. L. A. Hart, *Punishment and Responsibility* [Oxford: Clarendon Press, 1968], p. 10). I shall nevertheless speak of his theory as an attempt at reconciliation.

19. Cf. Ernest van den Haag, *Punishing Criminals* (New York: Basic Books, 1975), pp. 25–26; Andrew von Hirsch, *Doing Justice* (Westford, Mass.: Northeastern University Press, 1986): "[W]hile deterrence accounts for why punishment is socially useful, desert is necessary to explain why that utility may justly be pursued at the offender's expense" (p. 51); and Ten, *Crime, Guilt, and Punishment.* Ten adopts a "revised" compromise theory of punishment, the details of which needn't concern us here. Von Hirsch and Ten both take a pluralist approach, where both principles are given due weight.

made. Rawls's argument, which is seminal to the development of rule utilitarianism, has often been criticized as an incoherent version of utilitarian theory.[20] My point is different. It is that Rawls and others who have taken "the middle way," by focusing on the philosophical problem of how to defend utilitarianism against the retributive charge that it justifies punishment of the innocent, give an account of punishment that is untrue to our practice, to arguments actually made by practitioners. Retributivists do not justify only whom or how much we may rightly punish; some retributivists declare *that* we *must* punish, as Kant does with his soon-to-be-deserted-island example. Both retributivists and utilitarians offer accounts of why we punish at all (to express condemnation of blameworthy acts and mete out justice; to augment social utility); and both counsel us on what rules should guide us regarding the distribution of punishment within the practice. Sometimes we require *mens rea* to convict a defendant; many acts are made crimes because society regards these acts as morally wrong; in sentencing we generally try to fit the punishment to the moral gravity of the offense; and we allow for mercy and pardons. Although some of these features of our practice have been given utilitarian rationales, all accord unambiguously only with the retributive principle.[21] But sometimes we hold people accountable to a strict liability standard; we punish acts that are clearly not morally culpable (such as unknowingly selling adulterated food);[22] and in determining a criminal's sentence we sometimes take into account the threat of

20. Cf. Primoratz, *Justifying Legal Punishment*; Ten, *Crime, Guilt, and Punishment*.

21. On the point that utilitarians can offer no account of mercy or pardon, because these presuppose a wrong deserving punishment, see Primoratz, *Justifying Legal Punishment*, pp. 36–37; and Alwynne Smart, "Mercy," in H. B. Acton, ed., *Philosophy of Punishment* (London: Macmillan, 1969), pp. 212–28.

22. The example may be misleading, since many legal theorists call such an offense a "public welfare offense," which they distinguish from strict liability offenses. See Richard Wasserstrom, "Strict Liability and the Criminal Law," *Stanford Law Review*, vol. 12 (July 1960), pp. 731–45.

future harm posed by the criminal, regardless of the moral gravity of the offense of which he has been convicted. These features of our practice accord only with the utilitarian principle. Two principles are immanent in our practice; they pervade it through and through, and sometimes they conflict. By insisting that the retributivist speaks only to questions concerning the distribution of punishment, questions inside the practice, and that the utilitarian speaks only to the question of why we punish at all, Rawls and other compromise theorists fail to take seriously enough the claims of either the retributivist or utilitarian immanent critic, *both* of whom employ their distinct conceptions of why we punish at all to criticize or justify actions taken within the practice. By acknowledging that legal punishment is essentially contested, we are *forced* to take seriously both retributive and utilitarian immanent critics.

I believe (though I do not know how to go about proving) that legal punishment is not merely contested, conflict-ridden, or filled with inconsistencies, but that it is *essentially* contested.[23] There are several senses of "essentially contested," all of which I believe apply to the practice of legal punishment. When we say a practice is essentially contested we might mean that one doesn't adequately comprehend the practice unless one comprehends each of the essentially contested understandings. Each of these understandings is an essential part of an adequate comprehension of the practice. In this sense punishment is essentially contested, for if by punishment we understood only retributive punishment or only utilitarian punishment, our understanding would be deficient—it would leave out many features which both utilitarians and retributivists would have to admit are part of our present practice of punishment. To say that a practice is essentially contested might also be to say that the core of the practice is as up for grabs as the peripheries or boundaries of the practice.[24] In a

23. *x* is "essential" to *y* if lacking *x*, *y* would not be *y*.
24. On the idea of "core" and "periphery" with respect to prac-

practice that by this criterion is *not* essentially contested, there may be actions which some think appropriate to the practice and others think inappropriate, not properly part of the practice, not consistent with its purpose; but all will agree what that purpose is. By contrast, they will not so agree in a practice that by this criterion *is* essentially contested. In this sense, too, punishment is essentially contested. Utilitarians and retributivists do not merely disagree about whether this or that action properly belongs to the practice; they disagree about the fundamental purpose of punishment. A third meaning of essentially contested is "necessarily or inevitably contested." This is a very strong criterion, but still one by which punishment might be said to be essentially contested.

As a practice, legal punishment has underlying it some idea; it fulfills some purpose. But this purpose is realized, in the case of legal punishment and many other practices, only through the establishment of institutions, and there are important consequences following from the institutionalization of a practice. Some theorists have suggested that one such consequence is a perhaps inevitable tension between the original idea underlying the practice and the requirements imposed by the institutions needed to realize that idea. Hanna Pitkin distinguishes the institutionalized existence of practices, which she calls their "form," from the essential purpose or idea underlying these practices, which she calls their "substance."[25] For example, in the debate, in Book I of Plato's *Republic*, between Socrates and Thrasymachus regarding what justice is, Socrates refers to the idea (or substance) of justice, while Thrasymachus refers to what justice in its institutionalized existence has come to mean, namely, "the advantage of the stronger." Pitkin argues that both Socrates and Thrasymachus are talking about the same concept, justice, but that

---

tices, see James Griffin, *Well-Being: Its Meaning, Measurement, and Moral Importance* (Oxford: Clarendon Press, 1986).

25. Hanna Pitkin, *Wittgenstein and Justice* (Berkeley: University of California Press, 1972), p. 187; cf. pp. 186–92.

the conflict between the two reflects a typical process: when ideas or purposes become institutionalized, they become transformed. Justice takes on a new meaning. The original meaning is not lost, however; it is preserved and is in tension with the transformed conception.[26] Pitkin, then, suggests that the contested character of justice derives from the tensions that result when ideas and purposes are institutionalized. Such a process might account for the essentially contested character of legal punishment.[27]

Several theorists have argued that the original purpose of punishment was to mete out justice, which some think was originally manifested as the "primitive" urge to avenge.[28] Hegel notes that the German word for justice, *Gerechtigkeit*, is related to the German word for revenge, *Rache*.[29] Some argue that responsive attitudes underlie punishment: we punish as a response to blameworthy actions (in response perhaps to a "primitive urge," perhaps to an abstract conception of just

26. Cf. Pitkin, *Wittgenstein and Justice*, ch. 8. I do not mean to suggest that Pitkin thinks ideas come from nowhere. She describes two processes: from concept to practice, and vice versa.

27. Pitkin herself suggests the application to punishment in *Wittgenstein and Justice*, p. 188.

28. See Karl Menninger, *The Crime of Punishment* (New York: Viking Press, 1966); Hans von Hentig, *Punishment: Its Origin, Purpose and Psychology* (1937; reprinted Montclair, N.J.: Patterson Smith, 1973); Emile Durkheim, *The Division of Labor in Society*, trans. George Simpson (1893; reprinted Glencoe, Ill.: Free Press, 1933). René Girard, in *Violence and the Sacred*, trans. Patrick Gregory (1972; reprinted Baltimore: Johns Hopkins University Press, 1977) sees legal punishment as a functional equivalent to primitive sacrifice, which puts an end to the chain of revenge violence. Nietzsche says that the idea that the criminal deserves punishment came later; originally punishment's roots were in "anger at some harm or injury, vented on the one who caused it," but that this anger was "held in check" by the idea of paying back the injury through equivalent pain, an idea that has its roots "in the contractual relationship between creditor and debtor" (Friedrich Nietzsche, *On the Genealogy of Morals*, trans. Walter Kaufmann and R. J. Hollingdale [New York: Vintage, 1969], essay 2, section 4).

29. G. W. F. Hegel, *Vorlesungen über Rechtsphilosophie (1818–1831)*, ed. Karl-Heinz Ilting (Stuttgart-Bad Canstatt: Friedrich Fromman, 1973), vol. 4, p. 294.

deserts); and these responsive attitudes are not utilitarian. But we translate these attitudes into institutional contexts; once we have done this, utilitarian considerations force themselves upon us.[30] In this view, when punishment became institutionalized we of necessity became utilitarians (or at least consequentialists).[31]

But perhaps this is not the right story. It is difficult to say what is original idea or "core justification" and what is institutional consequence. Bentham argues the opposite. For Bentham, the original idea underlying punishment, its core justification, is utility. For Bentham, it is the demands on which retributivists typically insist that are institutional consequences. Bentham suggests that as a result of having a practice engaged in by many people, demands emerge for fairness, equal treatment, due process. One of these demands is that we punish only for acts stipulated by law as mischiefs. Once we codify laws as part of a practice—once we declare certain commonly occurring mischiefs to be crimes—the demand emerges that we punish only crimes; and Bentham implicitly acknowledges this retributive demand.[32]

No matter which story is right.[33] In either case the contested character of legal punishment arises from the interplay between ideas and institutional consequences.

30. Joel Feinberg argues this in *Doing and Deserving*, pp. 82–83.
31. As I argued in chapter 4, retributivism needn't be nonconsequentialist or deontic; the retributivist can acknowledge that institutions are required to attain her ideals at all and can therefore insist, as a condition of her retributivism, on the maintenance of the institutions, even if that requires violating the ideals.
32. See Jeremy Bentham, *An Introduction to the Principles of Morals and Legislation* (1789; New York: Hafner Press, 1948), ch. 15, section 25: in discussing the accidental punishment of a person innocent of an offense, Bentham uses the phrase "justly punished" to describe the punishment deserved by someone guilty of an offense. Bentham thus implicitly acknowledges the retributive principle that we may punish only those who commit offenses—justice demands this. But see Primoratz's discussion of Bentham, *Justifying Legal Punishment*, p. 26, for counterevidence.
33. An appeal to ordinary language might suggest that retribution is core and that utilitarian considerations emerged as institutional

5. Retributive Immanent Criticism in an Essentially Contested Practice

If I am right that legal punishment is an essentially contested practice, then the effort of contemporary theorists to bring together utilitarianism and retributivism by claiming that the two principles share in a division of justificatory labor, or that each is to be given due weight in a pluralist approach, is misdirected. Truth lies not in false reconciliation but in acknowledgment of incompatibility and difference.[34] But how will this truth help the practitioner of an essentially contested practice? The immanent critic uses the principle(s) underlying the practice as a guide for action within the practice. But if both utility and retribution are principles immanent in, indeed essential to, legal punishment, what is the immanent critic to do? Adherence to one principle implies a resolution to a practical problem that is precisely the opposite of the resolution implied by adherence to the other principle.

Of course, one possibility for the immanent critic of an essentially contested practice is to argue that the practice ought not to be essentially contested; for example, the retributivist can argue that punishment is essentially retributive and all aspects of the practice that violate that principle, such as plea-bargaining, extended sentences for repeat offenders, or use of a strict liability standard of accountability, should be stricken from the practice as inconsistent with its purpose, which is the condemnation of blameworthy action. The retributivist, in other words, can try to persuade us that retribution

---

consequence. It makes sense to argue that we can't punish someone who hasn't done a wrong (though ultimately this is an unconvincing argument). It would be far more odd to try to argue that when we punish someone convicted of a crime who is neither deterrable nor rehabilitatable nor a future threat, we really aren't "punishing."

34. There are still whole-hearted utilitarians (Jeremy Bentham and J. C. C. Smart, for example) and whole-hearted retributivists (Kant—with respect to moral, not legal, punishment; R. A. Duff; and Igor Primoratz). But their views, too, are inadequate, for they also fail to see that punishment is essentially contested.

is the core justification of legal punishment. In practice a defense attorney or judge wanting to justify, for example, acquittal for a crime lacking intent might argue just that: the point of punishing is to mete out justice, and where a wrong was done unintentionally, justice is not served by inflicting punishment.

But both competing principles are so deeply embedded in our practice and in our language that this argument, and in general the strategy of declaring legal punishment to accord with one principle and all aspects diverging from this principle no longer to be part of the practice, is unlikely to prevail as a rule. I believe we are stuck with our essentially contested practices. But rather than lament our fate of eternal disputation, I prefer to marvel at our ability to share a form of life that accommodates difference. For the fact that it *is* essentially contested might explain the *persistence* of a practice about which we are so deeply divided. The practice of legal punishment, just like the word "punish," gives expression to different voices while remaining a shared practice.[35] We are pulled toward two irreconcilable poles, both of which are incorporated into one practice. To say that legal punishment is essentially contested is to say that it is legitimate, or that there are good reasons, to be drawn to either pole. Both utilitarians and retributivists accept, if grudgingly, that actions guided by the principle of the other really are part of the practice.

It might be that an essentially contested practice persists precisely because it accommodates competing views to which we are strongly drawn. It does not accommodate conflicting principles by having each share in a division of justificatory labor; or by giving due weight to each principle—for example, by treating retributivism as a constraint on a utilitarian calculation; but by availing itself of an understanding of the practice as on the one hand utilitarian through and through, on the other hand retributive through and through. But because

35. Cf. Gallie's discussion of the concept of "champion" in "Essentially Contested Concepts."

both accounts of the practice are possible, neither is thoroughly persuasive. Neither a purely utilitarian nor a purely retributive practice of punishment would be acceptable to many of us. That it encompasses both principles *makes* the practice acceptable.

Suppose it is true that practices such as punishment are essentially contested in the strongest sense—"necessarily or inevitably contested." Of what use would knowledge of this be to those within the practice who must decide whether to do this or that? It would seem that practitioners are being told that there are, and always will be, good reasons to take either of two conflicting actions. Is there any value in knowing that not a single, self-consistent principle, but conflicting and at times irreconcilable principles, are immanent in (some of) our practices?

In one sense, gaining knowledge that a practice is essentially contested leaves the practice unchanged—two conflicting principles are still immanent in it; all that is different is that we now recognize this. But there is a sense in which this knowledge affects the practice. W. B. Gallie argues that though knowing a concept is essentially contested means we must live up to the fact that it's impossible to find a general principle for deciding which of two contested uses is best, it also means there are "intellectually respectable conversions," to be distinguished from those of "a purely emotional, or a wholly sinister kind."[36] Our knowledge might lead to a "marked raising of the level of quality of argument in the disputes of the contestant parties." Gallie suggests also that knowledge that a practice is essentially contested lets us exclude the "intrusions of lunatic voices."[37] Frank Michelman argues that awareness of fundamental contradiction is liberating:

> It is after all a crucial point about "the fundamental contradiction" that it is a form of order, not chaos. It signifies

36. Gallie, "Essentially Contested Concepts," pp. 184–85.
37. Ibid., pp. 188–89. Some of us might think this a very suspect goal: who gets to identify and exclude the "lunatics"?

not random confusion—as such ineffable, indescribable, unexaminable—but a formation of thought that can be named, perceived, cognized. And while surely there is nothing potentially enabling about the coming to consciousness of random disorder . . . appreciation of a hitherto denied contradiction can be emancipating.[38]

Both Gallie and Michelman are, I think, right to see an advantage in knowing that conflicting principles are immanent in a practice. The alternative against which we must judge the value of this knowledge is that we reject the demand that we be guided by any principle(s) and instead simply muddle through. Gallie and Michelman suggest that at the very least this knowledge focuses our debate. It also lets us see the *cost* there sometimes is of advocating one principle over the other. If the utilitarian and the retributivist can be persuaded that the practice of which they speak is essentially contested, they may shed a dogmatism that keeps them from acknowledging arguments with which they might concur were they not so steadfastly determined to consider only utilitarian or only retributive considerations. For example, with respect to the problem of whether we should legalize crack, the utilitarian who limits herself to the empirical issue of what the consequences of legalization would be fails to see the rather compelling point that perhaps we should want to make crack use illegal regardless of the consequences, because we regard crack use as wrong. Similarly, the diehard retributivist who takes the position "justice at all costs" fails to see that sometimes such a position is irresponsible: at times we simply must take consequences into account.[39]

Much of the debate regarding legal punishment has been characterized by self-conscious dogmatism. Bentham and Pos-

---

38. Frank I. Michelman, "Justification (and Justifiability) of Law in a Contradictory World," in J. Roland Pennock and John W. Chapman, eds., *Nomos*, vol. 28: *Justification* (New York: New York University Press, 1986), p. 86.

39. As the retributivist Duff writes: "I would act unjustly to prevent the heavens falling" (*Trials and Punishments*, p. 298).

ner both explicitly reject the idea that the criminal law embodies moral values or social judgments about right and wrong[40] and that we punish for reasons other than social utility or economic efficiency. Their accounts are unpersuasive precisely because they refuse to acknowledge a truth about our practice: we *do* insist on punishing the rapist or murderer, not on the basis of some calculation of social utility (either of punishing the particular rapist or murderer, or of as a rule punishing rapists or murderers), but because we regard rape and murder as abominable, as *deserving* our condemnation. Similarly, Kant, in his discussion of moral punishment, explicitly rejects not merely utilitarian but *any* consequentialist considerations. Kant's account, too, is unpersuasive, insofar as it refuses to acknowledge a truth about our practice: sometimes we must take consequences into account if we are to maintain the institutions that let us mete out justice at all.

We might think, given my view that both utility and retribution are principles immanent in punishment, that we should say there is no single practice of legal punishment, but a mixture of distinct practices, of retributive punishment and utilitarian punishment; and that what I offer in chapter 4 is an immanent criticism not of legal punishment but of retributive legal punishment. But in maintaining that legal punishment is an essentially contested practice, I mean that it is a single practice that has conflicting principles. The judge who refuses to accept a plea bargain on the principle of justice is not practicing "retributive punishment" but simply "punishment" as he understands it. The suspect brought into the station house to be questioned by the police and eventually to be tried before a judge, convicted, and sentenced to prison experiences *one* practice. The prosecutor, judge, parole officer, sentencing commission members, and prison warden all engage in one and the same practice; but there are conflicting interpretations

40. For Bentham, there is no such thing as right apart from that which is good or that which maximizes pleasure and minimizes pain. Cf. chapter 3, section 1.1, above.

of what that one practice is. Similarly, readers often disagree about their interpretation of a novel; but we say, not that each interpretation is of its own novel, but that they are different interpretations of one and the same novel.

By my declaring that the practice of punishment is essentially contested, that it has not one essential purpose but, rather, a set of not always consistent purposes, we might think that I am *defending* a combination of retributive and utilitarian approaches. But that is not my position. I defend the retributive interpretation of the practice, while acknowledging that the practice has immanent in it conflicting principles. The fact that a novel has more than one interpretation, and that I know this, needn't deter me from advancing a particular interpretation of the novel which I think is best. Similarly, that I acknowledge legal punishment to be a practice with competing interpretations, none being "correct," needn't deter me from favoring one in particular, and not merely on a whim, but because I have good reasons for thinking it is the best.

I hear and empathize with the cries of injustice and oppression of the marginalized who are punished for violating laws they don't regard as their laws; I would be outraged by the punishment of a person who lacked the mental capacity to know what he was doing in committing a crime; I am troubled by the use of plea bargains that fail to acknowledge the crime committed and instead profess to punish crimes not committed. I see hypocrisy in using the criminal justice system to keep a person behind bars not because of what he has done in the past but because society fears what he may do in the future. These judgments both draw on and ground my understanding of why we punish, an understanding that, while but an interpretation, I believe provides the best account of, and makes coherent, the complex but connected actions and institutions which constitute our practice of legal punishment.

To declare that legal punishment is an essentially contested practice needn't be completely to undermine our convictions and commitments, either to utilitarian, or, in my case, to retributive accounts of the practice. It is, rather, to acknowledge what seems to me an unavoidable, though perhaps disappointing, truth about the human condition: our practices lack absolute grounds, and their purposes can be established only by interpretation, about which we may disagree.[41] Given the strategic advantage for someone wanting to justify doing *y* for reason *x*, of being able to say we *already* do *y* for reason *x*, and so long as we are aware of the need sometimes to ask why we have our practices at all, to leave open the possibility of radical criticism, immanent criticism is a strategy well worth pursuing. But in a practice acknowledged to be essentially contested in the strong sense of necessarily or inevitably contested, the honest and perspicacious immanent critic can hope only to draw us to one of two legitimate poles, to win this or that battle, but never to prevail.

The observation that legal punishment is essentially contested is not merely a meta-theoretical, detached, empirical assessment of and prediction concerning discourse about punishment. It is meant to shape that discourse. I believe that the retributive account for which I have argued is stronger for being informed by this observation. By acknowledging that as a complex practice legal punishment incorporates conflicting values and fulfills competing purposes, the retributivist is forced to adjust her conception of the ideals of the practice so that it more adequately reflects the facts. By taking seriously the problems prosecutors, trial court judges, and other practitioners *actually* confront, the retributive immanent critic may have to rethink her ideals—"Do I really want to insist that we abolish plea-bargaining because it violates the retributive ideal, even though the practitioner insists that doing so will either lead to the collapse of the criminal justice system or else necessitate a clandestine system of bargaining that might

41. Cf. Charles Larmore, *Patterns of Moral Complexity* (Cambridge: Cambridge University Press, 1987), p. xi: "[W]e do best to see morality, at its deepest level, as a motley of ultimate commitments. As a result we should acknowledge that moral conflict can be ineliminable."

be even more objectionable?" But rather than giving up her ideals in the face of a nonconforming actuality, the retributive immanent critic who accepts the nonfoundationalist view of practices and who is therefore no longer dogmatically committed to her retributive ideals can with adjusted ideals persevere in the face of a less than ideal reality.

Appendix

In this appendix we shall consider practices in two very different societies, fifth-century Athens and the twentieth-century United States, practices which, while very different from each other in certain respects, we shall assume are both examples of the practice of legal punishment.[1] Our purpose is to see how in each case conflicting principles are immanent in the practice.

1. Athenian Homicide Law

When an Athenian was killed the reaction varied depending on the circumstances. Douglas MacDowell provides the following examples, which serve to illustrate the complexity of the Athenian practice of legal punishment. We may think of each of these examples as a subpractice.

> (1) If someone was accused of intentional homicide he would be tried at the Areopagos, a law court of special

1. One reason for my picking these two practices is that there happen to be excellent accounts of each which emphasize points important to my argument that the practice of legal punishment is complex and guided by competing and seemingly mutually exclusive principles. In this section I shall rely exclusively on two sources: on Athenian homicide law, Douglas M. MacDowell, *Athenian Homicide Law* (Manchester: Manchester University Press, 1963); on American criminal law, Sanford Kadish, *Blame and Punishment: Essays in the Criminal Law* (New York: Macmillan Publishing, 1987). All page numbers in the text of this appendix refer to one or the other of these works.

dignity and noted to be the least corruptible court (pp. 43–44). If someone was accused of unintentional homicide he would be tried at the Palladion, an outdoor court which heard what were regarded as less important cases (pp. 45, 69). Penalties for intentional homicide ranged from death or perpetual exile to confiscation of property, whereas for unintentional killers the laws would allow pardon and very sympathetic treatment (p. 110).

(2) If a victim forgave his killer, as could happen, for example, if the victim had just been given poison and was not yet dead, the killer would be immune from punishment (p. 8).

(3) Trials would be held for unknown or missing murderers, and animals or objects (such as a falling stone) that caused death (pp. 85–86). An offending object would be cast beyond the frontier (p. 86).

(4) When a person who committed unintentional homicide was granted a pardon by all the relatives of the victim or by ten members of the phratry (a clan based mainly on family relationship, p. 124), he could return from exile, but only after religious sacrifice and cleansing (p. 120).

(5) Athenians practiced "androlepsia," the taking of hostages to encourage extradition of killers not present in the state (p. 149).

MacDowell points out that no single principle can account for all of these aspects of the practice of legal punishment in Athens. He argues that three ideas lurked behind the practice: vengeance, cleansing (purification), and deterrence (p. 3, and ch. 14 passim); and that we can't know which idea was "most important" (pp. 142–43). Intentions matter (point 1), and this makes sense, argues MacDowell, only if deterrence was a prominent idea or purpose of the practice (p. 147). The distinction between intentional and unintentional homicide cannot readily be accounted for if we take the point of the practice of dealing with homicides to be vengeance or purification. The practice that if a victim absolved his killer no prosecution for homicide could follow (point 2) reveals, to MacDowell, that vengeance was a justification for punishing murderers. Such a practice could not be justified by deterrence or purification (p. 148). The practice that when an unintentional killer was pardoned and allowed to return from exile he had to be cleansed (point 4) is justified only by the purification idea (p. 148). Perhaps the practice of trying animals and "banishing" stones that had injured or killed (point 3) can also be justified on purification grounds, but perhaps this was done for the sake of vengeance; we don't know. But it was probably not done to deter (though even this is conceivable) (pp. 142–43). Finally, the practice of androlepsia (point 5) belies the purification idea, since the killer was not present to pollute the state (p. 149).

MacDowell infers that these contradictions suggest that the laws constituting Athenian practice in dealing with homicide were the product of more than one man: when the idea of pollution became current the law was amended, leaving behind inconsistencies (p. 150).

2. United States Criminal Law Doctrine

Sanford Kadish argues that some aspects of our criminal law can be accounted for only by a Kantian or rights-based theory, whereas others can be accounted for only by a utilitarian or consequentialist theory. The following examples are sufficient to show his point.

> (1) Law enforcement officials may justifiably kill an aggressor when they reasonably believe this necessary to prevent violent felonies and to apprehend any felon, and private persons may do the same in self-defense not only against imminent loss of life but also against kidnapping or forced sexual intercourse. No one may kill an aggressor solely to protect property, although a resident may kill someone who forcibly enters a dwelling (p. 111).
> (2) I may justifiably kill three terrorists to save my life (p. 122).
> (3) I may not justifiably kill the same three terrorists to save my life if I know that as I do so an innocent

bystander will also be killed (for example, if I use a gre-
nade to kill the terrorists, knowing that there is a person
in the next room) (p. 123).

(4) I may justifiably kill the three terrorists and the
one innocent bystander if the terrorists pose an imminent
threat to both myself and a companion (as opposed to
just myself) (p. 123).

(5) I am not legally obliged to save another's life, no
matter how easily I could do so (p. 113).

It's hard to find a single principle to account for all of these
aspects of our practice. That intentional killings of aggressors
are justified (point 1) cannot be readily explained by utilitarian
principles—utility does not explain why we may kill the ag-
gressor, nor why we may kill three (point 2) or twenty aggressors to save one life (pp. 116–17). Kadish suggests that the
justification of intentional killings of aggressors is based on a
theory of moral rights that claims the autonomy of the person,
and that this Kantian principle of the autonomy of the individual may account also for what I have indicated as point 5:
a requirement to save another person would collide with this
principle of autonomy (p. 128). In the cases in which bystand-
ers are involved (points 3 and 4), however, another principle,
that of choosing the lesser evil, is invoked, and Kadish associates this principle with utilitarian or consequentialist theories (p. 123). Kadish concludes: "I am dubious that any single,
self-consistent theory is likely ever to comprehend the whole
of our experience" (p. 129).

Bibliography

Alschuler, Albert. "The Prosecutor's Role in Plea Bargaining." *University of Chicago Law Review*, vol. 36 (Fall 1968).

Andenaes, Johannes. "General Prevention—Illusion or Reality?" *Journal of Criminal Law*, vol. 43 (1952).

———. *Punishment and Deterrence*. Ann Arbor: University of Michigan Press, 1974.

Armstrong, K. G. "The Retributivist Hits Back." *Mind*, vol. 70 (October 1961).

Arnolds, Edward, and Norman Garland. "The Defense of Necessity in Criminal Law: The Right to Choose the Lesser Evil." *Journal of Law and Criminology*, vol. 65, no. 3 (1974).

Baier, K. "Is Punishment Retributive?" *Analysis*, vol. 16 (1955).

Baldridge, Letitia. *The New Manners for the '90s*. New York: Rawson Associates, 1990.

Barnett, Randall. "Restitution: A New Paradigm of Criminal Justice." *Ethics*, vol. 87, no. 4 (July 1977).

Bayles, Michael. *Contemporary Utilitarianism*. Gloucester, Mass.: Peter Smith, 1978.

Beccaria, Cesare Bonesana. *An Essay on Crimes and Punishments*. Philadelphia: William P. Farrand and Co., 1809.

Benn, C. K. "An Approach to the Problems of Punishment." *Philosophy*, vol. 33 (October 1958).

Bentham, Jeremy. *An Introduction to the Principles of Morals and Legislation*. Originally published 1789. New York: Hafner Press, 1948.

Berns, Walter. "The Morality of Anger." Originally published in *For Capital Punishment*, New York: Basic Books, 1979. Reprinted in Hugo Bedau, ed., *The Death Penalty in America*. 3d ed. Oxford: Oxford University Press, 1982.

Brubaker, Stanley. "Can Liberals Punish?" *American Political Science Review*, vol. 82, no. 3 (September 1988).

Brunk, Conrad. "The Problem of Voluntariness and Coercion in the Negotiated Plea." *Law and Society Review*, vol. 13, no. 2 (Winter 1979).

Buckle, Suzanne, and Leonard Buckle. *Bargaining for Justice*. New York: Praeger Publishers, 1977.

Chambliss, William. *Crime and Legal Process*. New York: McGraw-Hill, 1969.

Chambliss, William, and Robert Seidman. *Law, Order, and Power*. Reading, Mass.: Addison-Wesley, 1971.

Davies, Thomas. "A Hard Look at What We Know About the Costs of the Exclusionary Rule: The NIJ Study and Other Studies of Lost Arrests." *Research Journal*, no. 3 (Summer 1983).

Dershowitz, Alan. "Who Decides and When?" In Gross and von Hirsch, eds., *Sentencing*.

Dolinko, David. "Some Thoughts About Retributivism." *Ethics*, vol. 101, no. 3 (April 1991).

Douglas, Jack, ed. *Understanding Everyday Life*. Chicago: Aldine, 1970.

Duff, R. A. *Trials and Punishments*. Cambridge: Cambridge University Press, 1986.

Durkheim, Emile. *The Division of Labor in Society*. Trans. George Simpson. Originally published 1893. Glencoe, Ill.: Free Press, 1933.

Dworkin, Ronald. *Law's Empire*. Cambridge, Mass.: Harvard University Press, 1986.

———. *Taking Rights Seriously*. London: Duckworth, 1978.

Epstein, Richard. *Takings: Private Property and the Power of Eminent Domain*. Cambridge, Mass.: Harvard University Press, 1985.

————. "A Theory of Strict Liability and Tort." *Journal of Legal Studies*, vol. 2 (1973).

Ewing, A. C. *The Morality of Punishment*. London: Kegan Paul, 1929.

Faris, Elsworth. "The Origin of Punishment." *International Journal of Ethics*, vol. 25, no. 1 (October 1914).

Feeley, Malcolm. *The Process Is the Punishment: Handling Cases in a Lower Criminal Court*. New York: Russell Sage Foundation, 1979.

Feinberg, Joel. *Doing and Deserving: Essays in the Theory of Responsibility*. Princeton: Princeton University Press, 1970.

————. "The Expressive Function of Punishment." *Monist*, vol. 49, no. 3 (1965). Reprinted in Feinberg, *Doing and Deserving*.

————. *The Moral Limits of the Criminal Law*. 4 vols. New York: Oxford University Press, 1984–1988.

Flew, Antony. "The Justification of Punishment." *Philosophy*, vol. 29, no. 111 (October 1954).

Foucault, Michel. *The Archaeology of Knowledge*, trans. A. M. Sheridan Smith. New York: Pantheon, 1972.

————. *Discipline and Punish: The Birth of the Prison*. Trans. Alan Sheridan. Originally published 1975. New York: Vintage, 1979.

————. *Language, Counter-Memory, Practice*. Ed. Donald Bouchard. Ithaca: Cornell University Press, 1977.

————. *Power/Knowledge*. Ed. Colin Gordon. Suffolk: Harvester Press, 1980.

Foucault, Michel, ed. *I, Pierre Rivière*. New York: Penguin, 1975.

Franklin, Mitchell. "The Contribution of Hegel, Beccaria, Holbach and Livingston to General Theory of Criminal Responsibility." In Edward Madden, Rollo Handy, and Marvin Farber, eds., *Philosophical Perspectives on Punishment*. Springfield: Charles Thomas, 1968.

Friedman, Lawrence. *Menninger*. New York: Alfred A. Knopf, 1990.

Gallie, W. B. *Philosophy and the Historical Understanding.* London: Chatto and Windus, 1964.

Girard, René. *Violence and the Sacred.* Trans. Patrick Gregory. Originally published 1972. Baltimore: Johns Hopkins University Press, 1977.

Goldstein, Abraham. *The Passive Judiciary.* Baton Rouge: Louisiana State University Press, 1981.

Gould, Stephen Jay. *The Mismeasure of Man.* New York: W.W. Norton, 1981.

Greenberg, David F., ed. *Crime and Capitalism: Readings in Marxist Criminology.* Palo Alto: Mayfield Publishing, 1981.

Griffin, James. *Well-Being: Its Meaning, Measurement, and Moral Importance.* Oxford: Clarendon Press, 1986.

Gross, Hyman, and Andrew von Hirsch, eds. *Sentencing.* Oxford: Oxford University Press, 1981.

Grupp, Stanley, ed. *Theories of Punishment.* Bloomington: Indiana University Press, 1971.

Hall, Stuart, Chas Critcher, Tony Jefferson, John Clarke, and Brian Roberts. *Policing the Crisis: Mugging, the State, and Law and Order.* London: Macmillan Press, 1978.

Hare, R. M. *Moral Thinking: Its Levels, Method and Point.* Oxford: Oxford University Press, 1981.

Harris, Marvin. *Cows, Pigs, Wars, and Witches.* New York: Random House, 1974.

Hart, H. L. A. "Prolegomenon to the Principles of Punishment." *Proceedings of the Aristotelian Society* (1959–1960). Reprinted in Grupp, ed., *Theories of Punishment.*

———. *Punishment and Responsibility.* Oxford: Clarendon Press, 1968.

Hart, Henry M., Jr. "The Aims of the Criminal Law." *Law and Contemporary Problems,* vol. 23 (1958).

Hegel, G. W. F. *Grundlinien der Philosophie des Rechts.* In Hegel, *Werke in zwanzig Bänden,* ed. Eva Moldenhauer and Karl Michel, vol. 7. Frankfurt am Main: Suhrkamp, 1970.

———. *Philosophische Propaedeutik.* In Hegel, *Werke in zwanzig Bänden,* ed. Eva Moldenhauer and Karl Michel, vol. 4. Frankfurt am Main: Suhrkamp, 1970.

―――. *Philosophy of Right*. Trans. T. M. Knox. Originally published 1821. London: Oxford University Press, 1952.

―――. *Vorlesungen über Rechtsphilosophie (1818–1831)*. 4 vols. Ed. Karl-Heinz Ilting. Stuttgart–Bad Canstatt: Friedrich Fromman, 1973.

Heritage, John. *Garfinkel and Ethnomethodology*. Cambridge, England: Polity Press, 1984.

Herzog, Don. *Without Foundations: Justification in Political Theory*. Ithaca: Cornell University Press, 1985.

Hobbes, Thomas. *Leviathan*. Ed. Michael Oakeshott. New York: Collier Books, 1962.

Holmes, Oliver Wendell. *The Common Law*. Boston: Little, Brown, 1923.

Jones, David. *Crime, Protest, Community and Police in 19th Century Britain*. London: Routledge and Kegan Paul, 1982.

Kadish, Sanford. *Blame and Punishment: Essays in the Criminal Law*. New York: Macmillan Publishing, 1987.

Kant, Immanuel. *Groundwork of the Metaphysic of Morals*. Trans. H. J. Paton. New York: Harper Torchbooks, 1964.

―――. *Lectures on Ethics*. Trans. Louis Infield. New York: Harper Torchbooks, 1963.

―――. *Metaphysik der Sitten*. In Kant, *Werke in Sechs Bänden*, ed. Wilhelm Weischedel, vol. 4. Originally published 1798. Darmstadt: Wissenschaftliche Buchgesselschaft, 1963.

―――. *On the Old Saw: That May Be Right in Theory But It Won't Work in Practice*. Trans. E. B. Ashton. Philadelphia: University of Pennsylvania Press, 1974.

Kaufman, Arnold. "Anthony Quinton on Punishment." *Analysis*, vol. 20, no. 1 (October 1959).

Kaufmann, Walter. *Nietzsche*. New York: Random House, 1968.

Kipnis, Kenneth. "Criminal Justice and the Negotiated Plea." *Ethics*, vol. 86, no. 2 (January 1976).

Kirchheimer, Otto, and Georg Rusche. *Punishment and Social Structure*. New York: Russell and Russell, 1939.

Krisberg, Barry. *Power and Privilege: Toward a New Criminology*. Englewood Cliffs, N.J.: Prentice-Hall, 1975.

Larmore, Charles. *Patterns of Moral Complexity*. Cambridge: Cambridge University Press, 1987.

Lenin, V. I. *The State and Revolution*. Peking: Foreign Language Press, 1976.

Mabbott, J. D. "Punishment." *Mind*, vol. 49 (1939), pp. 152–167. Reprinted in Grupp, ed., *Theories of Punishment*, pp. 41–57.

MacDowell, Douglas M. *Athenian Homicide Law*. Manchester: Manchester University Press, 1963.

MacKenzie, Mary. *Plato on Punishment*. Berkeley: University of California Press, 1981.

Mackie, J. L. *Persons and Values*. Oxford: Clarendon Press, 1985.

Marx, Karl, and Friedrich Engels. *Collected Works*. 44 vols. London: Lawrence and Wishart, 1975.

———. *Gesamtausgabe* (MEGA). Berlin: Dietz, 1975–.

Menninger, Karl. *The Crime of Punishment*. New York: Viking Press, 1966.

Michelman, Frank I. "Justification (and Justifiability) of Law in a Contradictory World." In J. Roland Pennock and John W. Chapman, eds., *Nomos*, vol. 28: *Justification*. New York: New York University Press, 1986.

Mill, John Stuart. *On Liberty*. Ed. Gertrude Himmelfarb. Harmondsworth, England: Penguin Classics, 1985.

Miller, Franklin G. "Restitution and Punishment: A Reply to Barnett." *Ethics*, vol. 88, no. 4 (July 1978).

Miller, Herbert S., William F. McDonald, and James A. Cramer. *Plea Bargaining in the United States*. Washington, D.C.: National Institute of Law Enforcement and Criminal Justice, Law Enforcement Assistance Administration, U.S. Department of Justice, 1978.

Morris, Norval, and Donald Buckle. "The Humanitarian Theory of Punishment: A Reply to C. S. Lewis." In Grupp, ed., *Theories of Punishment*.

Muir, William K., Jr. *Police: Streetcorner Politicians*. Chicago: University of Chicago Press, 1977.

Mundle, C. W. K. "Punishment and Desert." In Grupp, ed., *Theories of Punishment*.

Murphy, Jeffrie. "Marxism and Retribution." *Philosophy and Public Affairs*, vol. 2, no. 3 (Spring 1973).

Nardulli, Peter. "The Societal Cost of the Exclusionary Rule: An Empirical Assessment." *Research Journal*, no. 3 (Summer 1983).

Nehemas, Alexander. *Nietzsche: Life as Literature*. Cambridge, Mass.: Harvard University Press, 1985.

Nettler, Gwynn. *Explaining Crime*. 2d ed. New York: McGraw-Hill, 1978.

Nietzsche, Friedrich. *The Birth of Tragedy*. Trans. Walter Kaufmann. New York: Vintage, 1967.

————. *The Gay Science*. Trans. Walter Kaufmann. New York: Random House, 1974.

————. *Morgenröte*. Stuttgart: Alfred Kröner, 1964.

————. *On the Genealogy of Morals* and *Ecce Homo*. Trans. Walter Kaufmann and R. J. Hollingdale. New York: Vintage, 1969.

————. *Thus Spoke Zarathustra*. Trans. Walter Kaufmann. New York: Penguin, 1978.

Nozick, Robert. *Philosophical Explanations*. Cambridge, Mass.: Harvard University Press, 1981.

Packer, Herbert. *The Limits of the Criminal Sanction*. Stanford: Stanford University Press, 1968.

Pashukanis, Evgeny B. *Law and Marxism*. Trans. Barbara Einhorn. Originally published 1929. London: Ink Links, 1978.

Perkins, Rollin M. "Impelled Perpetration Restated." *Hastings Law Journal*, vol. 33 (November 1981).

Pilon, Roger. "Criminal Remedies: Restitution, Punishment, or Both?" *Ethics*, vol. 88, no. 4 (July 1978).

Piontkowski, Andrej A. *Hegels Lehre über Staat und Recht und seine Strafrechtstheorie*. Trans. from the Russian by Anna Neuland. Berlin: VEB Deutscher Zentralverlag, 1960.

Pitkin, Hanna. *The Concept of Representation*. Berkeley: University of California Press, 1967.

————. *Wittgenstein and Justice*. Berkeley: University of California Press, 1972.

Platt, Tony. "Prospects for a Radical Criminology in the USA." In Taylor, Walton, and Young, eds., *Critical Criminology*.

Posner, Richard. "An Economic Theory of the Criminal Law." *Columbia Law Review*, vol. 85, no. 6 (October 1985).

Primoratz, Igor. *Justifying Legal Punishment*. Atlantic Highlands, N.J.: Humanities Press International, 1989.

Quinney, Richard. "Crime Control in Capitalist Society." In Taylor, Walton, and Young, eds., *Critical Criminology*.

———. *The Social Reality of Crime*. Boston: Little, Brown, 1970.

Quinton, Anthony. "On Punishment." *Analysis*, vol. 15 (June 1954).

Radbruch, Gustav. "Die Überzeugungsverbrecher." In *Zeitschrift für die gesamte Strafrechtswissenschaft*, vol. 44. Berlin: Walter de Grunter, 1924.

Rawls, John. *A Theory of Justice*. Cambridge, Mass.: Harvard University Press, 1971.

———. "Two Concepts of Rules." *Philosophical Review*, vol. 64 (1955). Reprinted in Bayles, *Contemporary Utilitarianism*.

Ross, Laurence. "Law, Science, and Accidents: The British Road Safety Act of 1967." *Journal of Legal Studies*, vol. 2 (1973).

Rothman, David. "Decarcerating Prisoners and Patients." In Gross and von Hirsch, eds., *Sentencing*.

Rustigan, Michael. "A Reinterpretation of Criminal Law Reform in 19th Century England." In Greenberg, ed., *Crime and Capitalism*.

Sadurski, Wojciech. *Giving Desert Its Due*. Dordrecht: D. Reidel, 1985.

Sandel, Michael. *Liberalism and the Limits of Justice*. Cambridge: Cambridge University Press, 1982.

Schaar, John. *Legitimacy in the Modern State*. New Brunswick, N.J.: Transaction Books, 1981.

Schafer, Stephen. *The Political Criminal: The Problem of Morality and Crime*. New York: Free Press, 1974.

Schlesinger, Steven R. "The Exclusionary Rule: Have Proponents Proven That It Is a Deterrent to Police?" *Judicature*, vol. 62, no. 8 (March 1979).

Sharp, F. C., and M. C. Otto. "A Study of the Popular Attitude Towards Retributive Punishment." *International Journal of Ethics*, vol. 20, no. 3 (April 1910).

Smart, Alwynne. "Mercy." In H. B. Acton, ed., *Philosophy of Punishment*. London: MacMillan, 1969.

Smart, Barry. *Foucault, Marxism and Critique*. London: Routledge and Kegan Paul, 1983.

Smart, J. J. C. "Extreme and Restricted Utilitarianism." In Bayles, ed., *Contemporary Utilitarianism*.

———. *An Outline of a System of Utilitarian Ethics*. Adelaide, Australia: Melbourne University Press, 1961.

Smith, Steven B. *Hegel's Critique of Liberalism*. Chicago: University of Chicago Press, 1989.

Sutherland, Edwin, and Donald Cressey. *Criminology*. 8th ed. Philadelphia: J. B. Lippincott, 1970.

Taylor, Ian, Paul Walton, and Jock Young, eds. *Critical Criminology*. London: Routledge and Kegan Paul, 1975.

Ten, C. L. *Crime, Guilt, and Punishment*. Oxford: Oxford University Press, 1987.

———. "Positive Retributivism." *Social Philosophy and Policy*, vol. 7, no. 2 (Spring 1990).

Turk, Austin. *Political Criminality: The Defiance and Defense of Authority*, vol. 136. Sage Library of Social Research. Beverly Hills: Sage, 1982.

van den Haag, Ernest. *Punishing Criminals*. New York: Basic Books, 1975.

Vlastos, Gregory. "Socrates' Contribution to the Greek Sense of Justice." *Archaiognosia*, vol. 1, no. 2 (1980).

von Hentig, Hans. *Punishment: Its Origin, Purpose and Psychology*. Originally published 1937. Montclair, N.J.: Patterson Smith, 1973.

von Hirsch, Andrew. *Doing Justice: The Choice of Punishments*. Report of the Committee for the Study of Incarceration. Westford, Mass.: Northeastern University Press, 1986.

von Hirsch, Andrew, Kay Knapp, and Michael Tonry, eds. *The Sentencing Commission and Its Guidelines*. Boston: Northeastern University Press, 1987.

Walzer, Michael. *The Company of Critics*. New York: Basic Books, 1988.

———. *Interpretation and Social Criticism*. Cambridge, Mass.: Harvard University Press, 1987.

Wasserstrom, Richard. "Strict Liability and the Criminal Law." *Stanford Law Review*, vol. 12 (July 1960), pp. 731–745.

Wilson, James Q. *Thinking About Crime*. Rev. ed. New York: Random House, 1985.

Wittgenstein, Ludwig. *On Certainty*. Trans. Denis Paul and G. E. M. Anscombe. New York: Harper and Row, 1969.

Wootton, Barbara. "Diminished Responsibility: A Layman's View." *Law Quarterly Review*, vol. 76 (1960).

———. *Social Science and Social Pathology*. London: George Allen and Unwin, 1967.

Zimmerman, Don. "The Practicalities of Rule Use." In Douglas, ed., *Understanding Everyday Life*.

Index